BLACK GOLD OF THE SUN

BLACK GOLD OF THE SUN

Searching for Home in Africa and Beyond

Ekow Eshun

Illustrations by Chris Ofili

 PANTHEON BOOKS NEW YORK

Library of Congress Cataloging-in-Publication Data
Eshun, Ekow.
Black gold of the sun : searching for home in Africa and beyond / Ekow
Eshun; illustrations by Chris Ofili.
p. cm.
Originally published: London : Hamish Hamilton, 2005.
ISBN 0-375-42418-0
1. Ghana—Description and travel. 2. Eshun, Ekow—Homes and
haunts—England—London. 3. Ghanaians—Great Britain—Biography. 4.
Racially mixed people—Great Britain. 5. Eshun, Ekow—Travel—Ghana.
6. British—Ghana—Biography. 7. Ghana—Biography. I. Title.

DT510.2.E84 2006   16.6704'53—dc29   [B]   2005054370

www.pantheonbooks.com

For my family, Adelaide, Joe, Foriwa, Kodwo and Esi, with love

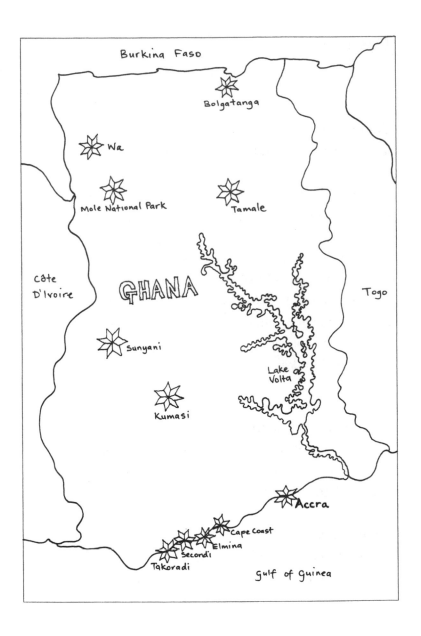

Contents

BLACK GOLD OF THE SUN

1

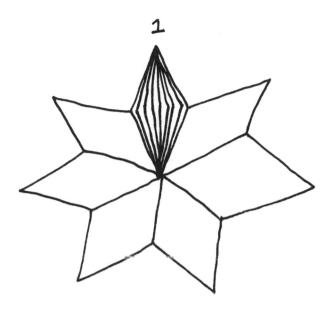

Thirty-five thousand feet over the Atlantic – Saturday night on Oxford Street – Boomerang – The night crawlers of Adabraka – Joseph Eshun and the Sugar Babies – An outstanding example of a tragic conflict

I

'Where are you from?' he said. 'No, where are you *really* from?'

It was the businessman who wanted to know. He'd been slumped beside me with his eyes shut and his mouth open since we'd left London. As the Boeing 777 dipped towards Accra he heaved himself up straight.

'Where are you from?' he repeated.

The overhead light glistened off the darkness of his skin. He wiped the film of sweat from his forehead.

I gave him the usual line.

'My parents are from Ghana, but I was born in Britain.'

In all the times I'd been asked the same question it was still the best answer I'd come up with. It wasn't a lie. It just wasn't the whole truth.

'Then you are coming home, my brother,' he said, leaning across me to empty a miniature of Teacher's Scotch into the plastic glasses on our foldaway tables.

'Akwaba,' he said, raising his glass. 'Welcome home.'

As we drained the whisky I thought of all the other ways I could have answered his question.

Where are you from?

I don't know.

That's why I'm on this plane.

That's why I'm going to Ghana.

Because I have no home.

I'd caught the plane that afternoon: a British Airways flight straight down the Greenwich Meridian line from Heathrow to Kotoka airport in Accra.

We'd risen above the clouds and, seated over the wing with the whine of the jet engines in my ears, I'd tried to concentrate on an anodyne movie about a gang of con artists breaking into the vault of a Vegas casino, before giving up to watch the plane's shadow ripple against the clouds below instead.

At Lagos, the flight made a stopover, and I caught my first glimpse of Africa since childhood. The sun was low and from out of the shadows ground crew in blue overalls hastened across the tarmac. A staircase thunked against the plane's flank. The doors sighed open. Tropical warmth filled the cabin. A stewardess with brittle make-up sprayed gusts of rose-scented insect repellent along the aisle.

'They treat us like animals,' grumbled the businessman.

A line of passengers in heavy cloth robes joined the plane, haloed with sweat. I compared their faces to mine. I looked as African as they did. But I didn't know how far that affinity stretched. Did it reach beneath the skin or did it end on the surface, in the slant of our eyes and the fullness of our lips?

It was April 2002, and I was thirty-three years old.

I was flying to Ghana to find out what I was made of.

My name is Ekow Eshun. That's a story in itself.

Ekow means 'born on a Thursday'. The Ghanaian pronunciation of it is Eh-kor and that would be fine if I'd grown up there instead of London where, to the ears of friends, Ehkor became Echo. Throughout my childhood I was pestered by schoolyard wags who thought it hilarious to call after me in descending volume: 'Echo, echo, echo.' It was my first lesson in duality. Who you are is determined by *where* you are.

My parents arrived in London from Ghana in 1963. They

never meant to stay. And even though they have spent most of the past forty years in Britain, Ghana is still their home. When I was a child growing up in London, its sounds and smells pervaded our house. Ghana was there in the hot pepper scent of palm nut soup tickling your nostrils as you entered the house; the highlife songs rising from the stereo; the sound of my mother shouting down a capricious telephone line to her sister in Accra.

But Ghana was their home, not mine. I knew this from experience.

I was born in 1968 in a red-brick terraced house in Wembley, north London. I was the youngest of four children. When I was two my parents moved the family to Ghana. We lived in Accra for three years. In 1974, we returned to London. I was five years old. I didn't plan to go back.

My last sight of the place was a country in meltdown. A military junta had taken power shortly before we left. I remembered long speeches by generals on a black-and-white television. The hourly price rises for a bag of rice. Strikes and shortages and demonstrations. What was there to return to?

I asked myself the question I'd been turning over since I first booked my flight: why make this trip?

During my late twenties I began to feel I couldn't live in London any more. The bigotries of the city weighed down on me. I saw condescension in the eyes of bank clerks and malign intent in the store detectives watching me from the end of an aisle. Lynch mobs chased me through my dreams. I fantasized about taking a machine gun to the streets.

From the extremity of my mood, I guessed that something more fundamental was at work than disaffection with the city. I knew my state of mind wasn't good. My fantasies were getting more violent. I needed to heal myself. I started to think about a childhood spent in London, then Ghana, then London again. Had I lost a part of myself in that toing and froing? Maybe by returning to Ghana I could become whole again.

Even though my roots were in Britain it was a white country, and I'd felt like an outsider there all my life. In Ghana I'd be another face in the crowd. Anonymity meant the freedom to be myself, not the product of someone else's prejudice. I bought a map of the country and studied its cities and rivers. I plotted a trip from the Atlantic coastline in the south to the dry north. I wanted to discover the whole country. I wanted to call it home.

I gave myself five weeks. I'd spend the first two exploring Accra, the capital. After that I'd travel west along the shoreline to Elmina, the town where Europeans first settled on African land in 1482. Then I could visit the neighbouring town of Cape Coast, Ghana's former capital, where my parents both grew up. That would take another week. In the remaining fortnight, I'd start heading north. I'd go to Kumasi, capital of the old Asante empire, in Ghana's central region. Then I'd keep going all the way through the arid northern plains until I reached the border with Burkina Faso.

By the time I was ready to go it was 2002 – twenty-eight years since I'd left the country as a child. I was looking for an antidote to London. I wasn't sure if that was too much to ask. All I knew was that if Ghana didn't live up to my hopes I'd have nothing left to hold on to. Then I really would be lost.

From Lagos the Boeing skirted the African coast.

I peered at the Atlantic, 35,000 feet below. This ocean had once been scattered with tall ships. Sails taut they had fought their way to Africa from Venice, Portugal and other states of Europe. Against the force of the northern trade winds masts had snapped. Boats had sunk. Men brave and timid had died. When they eventually succeeded in the fifteenth century it was no less an accomplishment than crossing the Sahara or traversing the Arctic. On 19 January 1482, a Portuguese fleet carrying 600 soldiers, masons and carpenters, holds filled with numbered blocks of granite, weighed anchor on the Ghanaian shoreline. At the town of Elmina they built São Jorge castle, the first permanent European settlement in Africa.

All along the west coast of Africa, Europe discovered riches. They named the land as they went – the Grain Coast, the Ivory Coast, the Gold Coast – and sailed home borne down with tusks and precious metals and the human cargo sometimes known as 'black gold'.

Yet the African connection to the western world was never simply passive. Among the Portuguese crew that landed at Elmina was the ordinary seaman Cristoforo

Colombo, for instance, who led Europe's discovery of the Americas ten years later accompanied by his African pilot, Pedro Nino.

The plane banked towards Kotoka airport and Accra hove into view, lambent in the falling light. Through the window I imagined the paths of the sailing ships preserved in the sea, forming a lattice of wake lines joining Africa, Europe, America and the Caribbean. It was impossible to tell where the connections began or ended. The shape of the continents themselves seemed to blur, as a result of centuries of commerce and migration, both voluntary and forced.

Kotoka control tower rose into view. Wheel hatches creaked open. The past is not history, I thought, as the plane screamed on to the runway. It beats against the present like the tide.

It was the smell that I first noticed – like rare orchids or rotten fruit.

Car horns blared in the distance. The lights of the terminal glowed across the tarmac. From the doorway of the aeroplane I followed the other passengers down the steps into a steam-room heat. I ploughed through customs, immigration and the scrum of porters wrestling me for my luggage, until I stood with my back to the airport, facing Ghana.

And Ghana stared back.

Behind a wire perimeter fence, wives and fathers and children playing hide-and-seek between the legs of their parents waited to greet the plane. There were smiles and waves as they spotted loved ones. None of them was there for me, but for a moment a wave of happiness engulfed me as I watched the crowd. Ghana wasn't home, but perhaps it would be possible for me to feel *at* home there.

Dragging my suitcase to the first car in a row of black-and-yellow taxis, I collapsed into the back seat. The cab shunted into traffic. Accra coalesced around me. The neon image of a grass-skirted dancer hovered above the roof of the hotel Shangri-La. Children materialized at traffic lights selling cigarettes and cellophane bags of iced water. Street hoardings advertised the virtues of Guinness Foreign Extra Stout and Richoco chocolate milk. Trucks rumbled by bearing ecclesiastical slogans above their windscreens such as 'Forward with God' and 'Shine, Jesus, Shine'. I smelled diesel fumes and sewage and, as the cab paused at a junction, the aroma of plantain and peanuts roasting on a brazier, the memory of which I'd savoured since my last taste twenty-eight years earlier.

From London, I'd arranged to borrow a house in a suburban neighbourhood called Upper Heights. It belonged to my mother's cousin who lived in Nottingham and spent only holidays there. Apart from Mrs Hagan, the housekeeper, I would be alone.

Upper Heights was a modern development of trim white houses built on a hill overlooking the city. Mrs Hagan, elderly, maternal, solicitous, had laid out a dinner of boiled yam and fish stew, with sliced mango and small hand-baked sponge cakes to follow. But the journey had left me exhausted. All I could do was stab at the food, then drag myself upstairs, Mrs Hagan clucking after me like a mother hen in case, as she seemed to think likely, I couldn't make it to bed before collapsing. Tired as I was, I couldn't sleep. Accra flickered before my eyelids in a sequence of dazzling impressions, as if I were gazing up at it on a screen from the front row of the cinema.

Nothing matches your first sight of a new city. You approach it with trepidation and its streets embrace you. The scent of bitumen and hot street food tantalizes your senses. Vendors and car horns and radios blare an unfamiliar rhythm. Your heart beats a noisy reply. That first night I gave up on sleep altogether. I sat on the balcony outside my bedroom looking at the mystery of the buildings glimmering in the distance. By contrast to London's pallor, Accra seemed to sparkle.

If I knew then as much as I do now, it's possible Ghana might still have appeared to shine. But first impressions are exactly that. There is an order of fact beneath them that is inescapable. After the sparkle fades you have to deal with what's left – whether you like what you see or not.

II

Saturday night on Oxford Street. Bright-eyed girls clung to the arms of broad-shouldered young men. Thrilled by the promise of the hours ahead, their eagerness lit the dark.

Couples hailed each other across the street, coalescing into groups that promenaded arm in arm along the pavement like a Broadway chorus line.

It was my cousin Kobby who suggested meeting on Oxford Street. I'd spent four days exploring Accra's markets and museums. Now I wanted to see it after dark.

'I know the perfect place,' said Kobby over the phone that afternoon. 'It's the most fashionable street in Accra.' But as I strolled along the pavement past the brightly lit bars and the gilded couples, my mind turned to what I'd read about the fashions of eighteenth-century Accra. How men of that era liked to tie little gold ingots into their beards and shave designs for ships or castles into their hair. And the care with which a woman would prepare herself each day: rubbing her body with perfumed oil, then mixing a fine white clay with water for make-up, which she'd press on to her face and bust with wood blocks shaped like circles or scimitars. As jewellery, she'd have worn bead necklaces made from coloured glass and gold bracelets hung with European coins such as the French louis d'or, gold rings and an anklet in silver, weighing a pound, on each foot.

She'd have worn a skirt of imported silk, secured with a belt decorated with keys and coins so that she jangled as she walked. Attached to her hair might have been a small gold bell or the red tail feathers of a grey parrot. In her house she would have kept a pet civet, and once a week she would use a small spoon to tap the secretions of its anal gland, which she would mix with water and dab on her neck as perfume.

During the same period, the secretions of the civet, a catlike mammal, were also being used by perfumers in France and England. History is full of unobserved parallels.

It was like that with Kobby and me. He'd come to London for the first time five years ago in 1997.

'This is your cousin,' said my mother. We'd shaken hands warily. Given he was a dozen years younger than me and had grown up a continent away, I wondered what we'd have in common. But Kobby turned out to be as hungry for music and movies as any child of the west. At seventeen, he was devoted to Tupac Shakur and WWF. I introduced him to Biggie Smalls and to Christopher Walken in *King of New York*. In return he offered stories about the trolls that were said to lurk in Ghana's woods and the spirits living in the lakes. At the end of his fortnight in London we shook hands again, this time more effusively. I hadn't seen him since.

Now I spotted him approaching along the neon-splashed street. Narrow-shouldered and light-framed as I remembered, but forcing his way through the crowds with his arms bowed as if he thought of himself as a heavyweight. We slapped each other on the back and Kobby led the way down the street.

'I don't live anywhere at the moment,' he said with an airy wave of his hand. 'I'm really too busy to think about a home.' He was a student now at the University of Ghana, but could rarely be found there.

At twenty-two he was also a senior copywriter at Ghana's leading advertising agency. Shuttling to meetings across the city in his black Volkswagen Golf, he would arrive at the agency offices only in the afternoon. From then he worked into the night scripting commericals and slept on the sofa beside his desk. Come morning he woke up and went to lectures. Kobby talked about launching his own small ads magazine. He said he'd been raising money to build a luxury car-wash site in East Legon. But he was cautious about revealing too many of his plans to me.

'No one knows the full scale of my affairs,' he said, drawing secrecy around him like an ermine.

What drove him to work eighteen hours every day? He already earned more than his parents combined, but listening to him it seemed the full scale of his affairs was bolder and less explicable than merely the accumulation of wealth. Kobby was waging a secret war, I realized, and the enemy was Ghana.

'When my parents retire I'll have to look after them,' he said. 'So I have to keep moving. I can't afford to stand still.'

His parents were teachers who lived in a bungalow in Cape Coast. As state employees their income had never recovered from the vicissitudes of the 1970s and 1980s, when inflation reached an annual rate of 100 per cent. Kobby and many of his friends had seen their parents cowed during those years. The memory had turned them into seditionaries plotting their own takeover of the state.

We turned off Oxford Street and entered a bar called @ The Office which was modelled on a real workplace. Mushroom-grey desks were arranged by the walls. The chairs were made of red moulded plastic. A shelf of yellow box files ran above the bar. The drabness of the environ-ment didn't seem to deter the crowd. Dressed in African-print shirts and army camouflage, they perched on the edge of the desks, drinking and flirting while a DJ played R Kelly, Jay-Z and Destiny's Child. The DJ's selection was the same as in any hip-hop or R & B club in London. Yet the crowd greeted each track with a familiarity that said it belonged to each and every one of them. For a moment I couldn't tell where I was.

I'd discovered hip-hop in the early 1980s, the era of Grandmaster Flash and Afrika Bambaataa. In those early formative years, the music marked the triumph of the unheard and overlooked. Black kids from the Bronx and Brooklyn banging their drums so loud the world stopped to listen. Hearing 'Planet Rock' in London for the first time at thirteen was like finding an answer to the isolation of growing up in a white suburb. The force of the music, its conviction, its lyricism, spoke to me. It let me know I wasn't alone.

But what did hip-hop say to the crowd here in Accra? Kobby returned from the bar with two bottles of beer. I remembered giving him a cassette of Tupac's *Me against the World* five years ago in London. He'd played it over and over, flipping the tape from side to side in ceaseless absorption. Tupac meant as much to him as Bambaataa had to me. And both of us had drawn the music from its source in America. London and Accra were links in a chain. We were the heirs to a legacy of Atlantic exchange that preceded us by centuries.

Kobby swept his hand across the bar. In the early 1990s, he said, the government liberalized Ghana's media laws. Dozens of radio stations sprang up across the country. Satellite TV stations beamed into the country from Germany, South Africa and the United States. The main beneficiaries of the broadcasting boom were the kind of young people gathered at @ The Office. The ones who had travelled to Europe and America, and returned seeking cultural rather than political change. Attuned to the music and fashions of the west they established themselves as a new hierarchy in broadcasting.

'A lot of the DJs on Joy, Vibe and the other radio stations are in their twenties,' said Kobby. He himself was the youngest advertising creative in the city. On Accra's radio stations you could hear US hip-hop and UK garage. On television, you'd find Brazilian tele novellas, Australian soap operas, African-American sitcoms, Manchester United matches, Japanese cartoons and Bollywood movies.

I bought another beer for each of us. We clinked our bottles and, as we did, it seemed to me that we were drinking to the polyglot Accra before us in the bar, within which all dreams were probable.

Some time later I found myself riding in Kobby's Golf towards a nightclub called Boomerang. In the back seat were two girls he'd met for the first time that evening in some unspecified way. I gazed out of the window, listening to them bat sarcastic remarks back and forth in pidgin English, the private slang of young Ghanaians. When

Kobby fell silent to negotiate the traffic, the girls sent text messages to their friends, who were apparently also riding towards the club in the backs of other cars. The messages, I imagined, were a running account of their sensations as they related to our car journey, their love affairs and hopes for the future, and the state, in abstract, of the turning world. Gathered together, these would have formed a telemetry registering the emotional state of Accra's young female population, a green flash on a hand-held screen signalling crisis or elation as the cars swept in loose formation through the night.

Kobby and I had bought another few bottles of beer before leaving the bar. I was halfway to drunk and it seemed to me there couldn't be a finer place than Accra at 1.37 in the morning, the road ahead clear and the city flowing in silence around the car. We arrived at Boomerang to find a swarm of cars descending on the club. In the flare of headlights I thought of aeroplanes morphing from distant stars to brute metal as they screamed to a landing. Around us sleek couples unfolded themselves from the cabins of Mercedes sports coupés. They emerged warily, shading their eyes as if they were gazing down on the scene from the top steps of their Learjet.

I followed them into the club and came to a dance floor overlooked at the far end by a neon-lit bar. An overhead monitor streamed videos of rappers waving $100 bottles of Cristal champagne. In imitation of the videos, the young men at the club were dressed in African-American labels such as Sean John and Fubu. The women wore outsize

Fendi sunglasses on their foreheads. From their shoulders swung handbags embossed with the monograms of Gucci and Louis Vuitton.

For all the vibrancy of the club, the booming sound system and the packed dance floor, I found it hard to enjoy myself. Where @ The Office, with its young people in African prints, braided hair and army camouflage, had seemed like a particularly Ghanaian response to the universality of hip-hop, Boomerang marked its wholesale embrace. In place of individuality there was a reliance on brands and labels that made my heart sink. You could walk into a club in London, New York, Kingston or anywhere else that black people gathered on a Saturday night and find a crowd dressed with the same kind of ostentation. It was as if we had taken our cues from music videos and magazines to learn how to dress, how to hold ourselves, how to articulate what it meant to be black. We had become consumers of our own image.

I let Kobby and the girls disappear on to the dance floor without me, while I stood at the bar nursing a sour mood. Yet the truth, I realized when I was alone, was that Boomerang was as 'authentic' as any other facet of the night-time city. Just because it didn't conform to my expectations of an African club didn't make it any less real. In actuality, what was disturbing to me wasn't the club so much as the gap between what was in front of me and what I held in my head.

For the past twenty-eight years I'd carried a mental picture of Ghana frozen in the early 1970s. When I thought of the country, I saw passers-by in Afros, heard highlife music blaring from the radio and envisioned my uncle Abousom cruising the streets in his yellow-and-black Ford Capri. Somehow I'd imagined nothing would have changed. Instead I'd returned to a city of SUVs, mobile phones and hip-hop clubs. The transformation made my memories seem false. I felt like an interloper.

Ghana had tilted towards the Atlantic world in my absence. I'd seen the indications of it all evening. The momentum was irrevocable. And it struck me, too, that there were moments when it was futile to dwell on those changes too deeply – chiefly when everyone else seemed to be having a good time. I floated towards the dance floor, giving myself over to the music and the beat of the night.

III

As dawn approached, the hustlers and the night crawlers, the whisky-soaked and the drug-addled, dragged themselves to Adabraka in the hope of a last carousal before morning. The neighbourhood lay on top of a hill in central Accra, commanding a low but distinct view across the city. At the base of the hill, prostitutes huddled in the arc-lit forecourt of a Mobil petrol station. Cars drew up beside them. The women stuck their heads inside so that they were visible only from the waist down, skirts stretched tight over heavy thighs. They negotiated a fee and got into the front seat. The car accelerated, rear lights vanishing into the gloom. From the unlit edges of the forecourt, the women's pimps watched the trade. Slouched against a row of cars, they wore gold chains and a uniform expression of severity. The red tip of a cigarette glowed in the darkness. A quarter bottle of brandy was passed from hand to hand.

Beneath the arc lights, the roof of a parked car stood open. A group of the women was dancing to the music uncoiling from its radio. As I rode by in Kobby's car I spied them for a frozen moment. With almost unbearable poignancy, their levity struck me as belonging to another, more benign place, quite distant from the forecourt and the gaze of the pimps who stood in the shadows, regarding them with contempt.

As we ascended the hill the street became darker and more still.

We passed a scattering of poorly lit bars. Fugitive shapes flitted beneath streetlights. Without warning a naked man stumbled into the beam of our headlights. His hair was matted into dreadlocks. A pair of tablespoons clattered on a string around his neck. Oblivious to our presence, he stood mumbling to himself, then disappeared down a side street in search of a way to feed his addictions.

The top of the hill was crowned with bars. Their tables lined the street. Music drifted into the warm night air. We found a seat and ordered a drink. Most of the customers at the bars looked as if they'd spent the night working: selling drugs or selling themselves, or in the case of a few spectral figures begging for change among the tables, simply trying to distinguish reality from their own unruly imaginings.

Yet the tensions of the night were beginning to leaven. Even the most severe-looking pimps were smiling. Shortly the sun would rise. The daytime business of the city would begin again. From the tower of a mosque somewhere below came a call for the start of dawn prayers.

Barmen began collecting chairs from the pavement. Kobby left and, sitting alone, I sipped at a bottle of beer. As I did so my thoughts turned to Joseph Eshun, my grandfather, ninety-five years old, with a crown of white hair and the profile of a bird of prey.

Whenever he visits Britain, wearing a lambswool scarf round his neck in my parents' overheated living room, Joseph tells me about the parties and balls he used to attend in 1930s Cape Coast. Through his words I see him scraping his hair into a centre parting and rubbing Pond's Cold Cream into his cheeks. He puts on his stiff-collared white shirt and his evening suit with its silk lapels. The local children have gathered outside the gates of Cape Coast Town Hall. Joseph pushes through them. He enters the hall. The Sugar Babies, the great dance orchestra of their day, are playing a waltz. As he glides on to the floor with a partner, Joseph's patent shoes sparkle with the reflection of the chandelier that hangs above the ballroom.

This was his world on a Saturday night. But Joseph the ballroom dancer was also by day headmaster, storekeeper, barman, optician and football club chairman. A photograph from the 1930s shows him in a two-piece suit and spats. A jewelled pin glints on his tie and his aquiline nose is tilted towards the sky. From the picture, it's easy to imagine him walking through town nodding to calls of 'Master Eshun', the title conferred on him as head teacher of Cape Coast's Zion School.

In 1877 Britain had moved the capital of the Gold Coast from Cape Coast to Accra, but the signs of colonial presence are found still in street names such as Beulah Lane, Victoria Park, Coronation Street and London Bridge, with its bust of a grim-faced Queen Victoria. Joseph's home stood in the market district of Kotokuraba. It was built around a central courtyard with individual apartments for family members and their children. At the front of the house, facing the busy street, he opened a store that sold tinned food and dry goods. In the back, he put a bar where he served Club, Star and the other Ghanaian beers, along with Scotch whisky and London gin.

During the late 1930s, a German named Herr Oppenheim set up business in Cape Coast. Joseph, perennially curious about life beyond Ghana, struck up a friendship with him. He invited the German to stay in his apartments on the second floor of the compound, where the two men talked late into the night about the state of the world. When war broke out Herr Oppenheim returned reluctantly to Germany. In parting he left his friend the machines of his trade – which was how, in addition to being headmaster and barman, Joseph became Cape Coast's sole optician. Patients came to him as they had to Herr Oppenheim.

They sat on a wooden chair in his living room, and he shone an ophthalmoscope into their eyes to check the condition of their retinas and optic nerves. Foot-long tubular packages would arrive from the British-American Optical Company of London. He'd unwrap rows of lenses waiting to be ground into shape on his lathe, once he'd stripped their brown-paper packaging.

On Sundays, Joseph chaired team meetings of the Sparts football club. Downstairs in the courtyard the young men of the team would warm up, as they prepared for another match against their arch rivals, the Venomous Vipers. There was always commotion in Joseph's house and in that way it resembled the restless turning of its owner's spirit.

It was from my grandfather that I first heard mention of William Essuman-Gwira Sekyi. The two men had moved in the same social circle of balls and masonic lodge meetings. But Sekyi was older and grander than Joseph, a lawyer who became one of the first Ghanaians to question the link between civilization and colonialism until then taken for granted by Cape Coast's upper classes. Born in 1892, the son of a wealthy merchant, Sekyi went to a small Church school run by an English head teacher, where he was called by the Anglicized name of William Sackey. He wore a high collar and frock coat, and received lessons in English history, Latin, etiquette and elocution. At nineteen he was sent by his parents to England, to study law at University College, London.

From the deck of the steamer Sekyi waved to his family, excitement churning his stomach as the ship drew away from Cape Coast towards the grey Atlantic. At Plymouth, he boarded a train for the first time. Villages and ancient woods flashed past the windows. He imagined his journey as a royal progress, the land itself bowing in his presence.

As he wrote later of his travels, it seemed to Sekyi that he ascended to a higher order of existence by arriving in Britain. During his first days in the capital, he walked the streets in wonderment, gazing up at the sight of Westminster Abbey, the Tower of London, the dome of St Paul's rising before him against a pellucid sky. But as the months progressed his excitement began to dim.

With winter, the sky grew dismal. Trash whorled in the streets and mud clung to his trousers. He dreaded the bland meats served at his boarding house. The English themselves he regarded with distaste, as pallid, slump-shouldered and stinking of carbolic soap.

Yet with rising horror Sekyi was also realizing how England saw him. At college balls, girls exchanged sardonic glances when he requested a dance. In the dosshouses where he did volunteer work, the down-and-outs sniggered at his tailored suits.

'Where does a monkey get such nice clothes?' they said, laughing out loud so he could see their scarlet gums.

When he was invited to dinner, Sekyi came to expect the same questions: Did you wear clothes before coming to England, Mr Sackey? Is the climate safe for civilized people? Do they *eat* people in your part of Africa, Mr Sackey?

His degree finally completed at the end of three years, Sekyi returned to Cape Coast. Radicalized by his experiences in London he refused to be known by his Anglicized name any longer. Instead of English, he now spoke Fante in public. He wrote a succession of essays and a satirical play mocking the colonial fixation of the town's upper classes. Sitting at his desk in the evenings, his thoughts turned often to the events of his journey home from London.

It was 1915. As his ship steamed across the Atlantic it was torpedoed by a German U-boat. The vessel started to list, and the captain gave the order to abandon ship. Panic broke out among the passengers. In the mêlée Sekyi managed to clamber into a lifeboat. Others simply dived into the sea. Screams twisted up from the water. Behind him in the boat an Englishman with mutton chops and a red face was shouting. In the commotion, it took some time for Sekyi to realize he was the one being addressed.

'How dare you stay in this boat when English lives are in danger,' called the red-faced man. 'Get out at once and make room for a gentleman.'

Sekyi's head rang. He tried to reply, but the words caught in his throat. Water slapped at the sides of the boat. He stayed where he was. Passengers clambered into the lifeboat. Sekyi helped them in. They huddled together, staring at the ship as it started to sink. With it, the last of Sekyi's love for England descended to the ocean floor.

What would William Sekyi make of the modern Ghana I had seen that night. The Ghana of Jay-Z records, Mercedes coupés and Louis Vuitton handbags?

For all that he came to loathe London, his true anger was reserved for the Cape Coast elite and its mimicry of the English. His beliefs helped to galvanize the self-rule movement that led, in 1957, to Ghana's independence.

Yet embracing Africa didn't necessarily mean rejecting the west. At home Sekyi could be found with a cigar and a glass of wine listening to Wagner on his phonograph. His critics were perplexed by this apparent dichotomy. He was considered, wrote his son Henry Van Hein Sekyi, to be an 'outstanding example of a tragic and unresolved conflict, desiring at once to be pagan and Christian, aboriginal and European ... traditionalist and western progressive'.

Sekyi himself, however, perceived no contradiction in his character. Identity, he believed, was fluid not fixed, and I can see his shadow on men such as my grandfather and my cousin Kobby, both of whom understand Ghana to be a place of shifting possibilities. From his home in Cape Coast Sekyi walked down to Ghana's Atlantic shore. Finding himself between the land and the sea he chose to face both ways.

I drained the last of my beer and placed the bottle on the table. The bar was shutting. The street had emptied.

I walked down the hill into the wakening city.

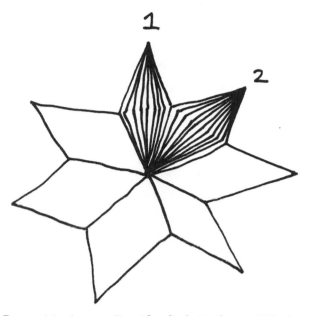

Burenyi in Accra – Esi, Elizabeth Taylor and Block O –
Malcolm X and Muhammad Ali in Accra – The pierrots of
Independence Square – Ants – Joe and Adelaide at the
Happy Bar – Joe vanishes – Adelaide alone – The Eshuns
depart for London

I

Soon after moving into Upper Heights I discovered that
my standing in the neighbourhood hovered somewhere
between prize pig and village idiot. When I lived in Ghana

as a child I spoke fluent Fante. It is the language of my parents and one of the most prominent of Ghana's seventy-five different tongues. I still understood Fante, but growing up in London left me no longer able to form the words needed to express myself. Ghana is a former British colony, and most people speak good English, so I hadn't anticipated trouble making myself understood. Yet without the ability to address them in their own language, I found I'd been rendered dumb.

Each evening as she laid the table for dinner, I saw a look of boundless compassion in Mrs Hagan's eyes. Disregarding my insistence that I understood Fante, she'd ask me about my day in the deliberate tones of a parent spooning mush to their baby. Precious, her niece, lived nearby and often came to visit. At those times the women stood over the table, discussing in Fante my appetite and mood, and what I'd done that day, while I sat between them, mutely spooning a bowl of groundnut soup.

On Upper Height's main street the neighbourhood housewives, returning from the market carrying woven baskets of cassava and tilapia fish wrapped in greaseproof paper, would speculate about my identity as I walked by. I was an African-American tourist; Mrs Hagan's retarded grandson; a Ghanaian who'd been to Abora Kyir (England) and come back with a swelled head and a phony accent. And who was I really? Even if I'd been able to answer to them in Fante, what would I have said?

At the end of the street stood Maa Lizzy's, the grocery store, where the local youth liked to gather after school.

They'd fall ostentatiously silent when I was sighted approaching. But in the time it took for me to be served by the affectless teenage girl behind the counter, word would flash round the neighbourhood. On the first such occasion, what seemed like a herd of kids galloped to the store for a look at me. Smaller children hoisted themselves on to the shoulders of big brothers for a better view. An ice-cream boy riding past parked his bicycle and began hawking ice lollies and tubs of sweet frozen milk to the crowd. Scuffles broke out at the back among those denied a decent view. It was a carnival, and I was the main attraction.

As I emerged into the light, someone shouted, 'Burenyi.'

Another voice called out the same word. Then they were all chanting it.

'Burenyi.'

'Burenyi.'

They trailed me down the street shouting, until one of the youngest children, a girl with hair in bunches like Mickey Mouse ears, tripped over at the front of the procession.

In the commotion that followed I slipped back home, where Precious was making soup in the kitchen.

'What does *burenyi* mean?' I asked.

She looked up from the stove.

'Where did you hear that?' she said.

'Nowhere,' I shrugged, trying to sound offhand. 'Just out today.'

Precious sprinkled pepper into the soup.

'It means "white man",' she said. 'Why do you ask? I thought you said you understood Fante.'

II

When I was twenty I met a girl called Hannah.

We fell in love.

It didn't last.

She was on my mind the morning after the kids called me a white man in Upper Heights.

The children's reaction brought home the fact that I was alone in a strange country. Hannah would have said that I courted loneliness. If that's the case, it's nothing of which I'm proud.

We were together for eighteen months – hardly an eternity, but enough time to know each other well. That was when it got difficult between us. Hannah had told me all about her friends and her parents and her childhood. She expected me to do the same. Only I didn't reveal anything to her about my past. The fate of our relationship came down to the reason why this was so. She said I didn't want to. I said I couldn't.

The last time I saw her was in an over-lit pub in Finsbury Park.

'I've noticed something,' said Hannah. 'You never get angry. You never get upset. It's as if you're never really here. You're so cut off from yourself it's impossible to reach you.'

'I care about you.'

'I'm not sure that's enough for me any more.'

'You don't want me?'

'I just want to know what you want.'

A cloud of cigarette smoke from across the room drifted past me. I noticed the ceiling was the colour of spoiled milk and the table was embedded with the ancient rings of beer glasses.

We'd had the same conversation several times before. In response to her questions, I used to tell Hannah I couldn't recall much about my childhood. The truth was different, though: I just couldn't remember anything I wanted to talk about. When I looked up at Hannah, her face seemed indistinguishable from childhood enemies such as Kevin Dyer and Dwayne Hall – the kids who'd conspired to humiliate me when I was at school; she was doing the same now.

'What do you know?' I said. 'You sit there like you've got all the answers, but you don't know a thing about my life.'

I said a lot more, most of it made incoherent by anger and shame. Hannah simply let me speak. When I finally exhausted myself, she sat for a while, twisting a lock of hair between her fingers.

'That's exactly my point. If I don't understand, why don't you try talking to me? I won't laugh at you or whatever it is you're scared of. I just want you to be yourself. Help me understand.'

The choice couldn't have been plainer: trust Hannah

enough to take her into my past or turn away into solitude. At the time it felt as if there was only one possible decision. Even years afterwards, when I'd recall the curve of her hips in bed beside me or the depth of her brown eyes, even then it didn't occur to me I might have done anything other than leave the pub that night by myself.

I've had relationships with several women since Hannah, but solitude remains more familiar to me than intimacy. I live by myself in a flat near the City of London. After the office workers have left for the night, a stillness takes hold of the streets, one that's punctuated occasionally by the sight of a vixen, two cubs yowling behind her, as they make their way to Bunhill Fields burial ground on City Road, to lie together near the grave of William Blake.

Nearby on Brick Lane, immigrants have been coming to make their home in London for hundreds of years. French Huguenots, Jews, Somalis, Bangladeshis – all in turn have built a community there and left an indelible mark on the neighbourhood. That's not my way. I prefer the in-between places – a flat above a row of shops; a cul-de-sac; the anonymous expanse of a council estate. Some place without an identity of its own where no one asks where you're from.

Yet I still woke up the morning after the incident at the store weighed down with the sense of my aloneness. I rang my sister Esi from the balcony outside my bedroom. When I first decided to return to Ghana, she talked about coming with me. But the more we discussed it the less enthusiastic she became. Esi is a year older than me. Her memories of the place were more vivid. She said she wasn't ready to go back to them.

'I never felt at home there,' said Esi, down the phone line. 'Do you remember that set of flats where we lived in Accra? Community One housing estate, Block O. With a big O painted on the side. These two boys would chase me around the courtyard there. I guess one of them liked me. But they called me "Guinness". I didn't understand what that was supposed to mean but there was obviously some racial undertow to it – I didn't have the right accent or I didn't fit in. And they used that against me.'

A mosquito buzzed around my head. I smacked it away and set off a ringing in my ear. Static surged along the phone line. For a moment Esi was submerged beneath its waves. Then her voice bobbed back to the surface.

'There was a funeral for an auntie of ours. She'd died of septicaemia after giving birth to her sixth child. But everyone said she was killed by a curse. On the day of the funeral the yard behind her house was filled with drumming and women ululating. The sound started to send me into a trance. I can't explain it exactly. Even at six I knew that certain types of drumbeats would make me drift away from myself. You start to dissolve. Your spirit gets drawn out of you until there's nothing left. I could feel it happening. It was terrifying. I ran as far from the sound as I could because I knew that if I didn't I would lose myself and disappear.'

I was listening to Esi speak, but for a moment all I could think of was how I used to creep into her room at night in London when we were kids. A pile of books lay on the floor beside her bed. Enid Blyton's *Mallory Towers*, *The Hobbit* and, at the bottom, the *Encyclopaedia of Epic Films*, a giant volume that claimed to 'capture in glorious detail all of Hollywood's greatest historical movies'. Esi was the book's oracle. She'd imbibed every scene of every movie. When I couldn't sleep I'd wake her up and we'd leaf through pictures of the chariot race in *Ben Hur*, the flaming ship taking Tony Curtis to Valhalla at the end of *The Vikings* and Elizabeth Taylor as Cleopatra, borne into Rome on a golden sphinx.

As it rose from her bed, Esi's voice was grave. She talked about the pictures as if she'd lived through ancient times and was recalling now those former years. As if she'd already seen too much at ten years old.

'When we first went back to Ghana Mum and Dad took us to see a fortune-teller,' said Esi. 'He was an old man with red robes and red eyes. He made us throw cowrie shells so he could read our future. He pointed to you and said, "Fine." Then he looked at me. He shook his head. "Her? No."

'I was going to have a terrible life. I was five years old. How could he say something so cruel? Mum and Dad took me back to see him, and he changed his prediction – I suppose on their insistence. But it was already too late. After that it felt like I couldn't touch anything without it turning to ash.

'In Block O we had a Labrador puppy called Husky. He was very cute, but completely unruly. When I played with him I forgot how strange it felt being in Ghana. But Husky's barking used to really irritate the neighbours. They complained to Dad and he decided Husky had to be put down. Some men from the north were hired to come and deal with the dog. Everyone said the reason they hired themselves as dog killers was because they liked to eat them afterwards.

'There were three of them who came, tall and silent, with scarification marks on their cheeks. They carried a machete each and an empty brown sack. They chased Husky round the courtyard. His feet were scrabbling on the concrete as he tried to escape. The men cornered him. Husky was wailing. They raised their machetes. I couldn't bear to watch any more. Just before I turned away I saw some fleas jump from his fur and splatter themselves red against the white wall.'

Esi's voice drowned in a fizz of static. The phone line died.

In the distance, sunlight beat off Accra's tall buildings. I stayed on the balcony till the evening. Underneath, the shadows of banana trees stretched gradually thinner until they vanished into the gloom of the evening. Nothing stirred. In the dark I felt like Laika the space dog, spinning above the earth while longing for a scratch between the ears.

III

The following day I rode into Accra on a tro-tro – one of the customized minibuses which serve in place of public transport throughout Ghana. When it became stuck in traffic I pulled out a guide book and discovered that Ghana had been a voguish destination for African-Americans in the 1960s. Having won independence from Britain in 1957, the former crown colony of the Gold Coast had become, after Sudan, only the second African country south of the Sahara with a black leader. For visiting Americans, the new nation was a powerful inspiration in their own prolonged struggle for civil rights. In 1962 Malcolm X spent a week in Accra engaged in meetings with the Ghanaian government, his trip coinciding by chance with a visit by Muhammad Ali. Their arrival was recorded for the *Ghanaian Times* by the writer Maya Angelou, one of a community of 200 black Americans living permanently in the city. The most distinguished of the expats was the veteran civil rights activist W. E. B. DuBois, who'd renounced his US passport for Ghanaian citizenship at the age of ninety-three. All of these recent arrivals were preceded, however, by Louis Armstrong, who'd visited the Gold Coast in 1956, a year before the formal handover of power, and played to a crowd of 100,000 at the Accra racecourse.

It was a heady time in the country's history, much of it embodied by Kwame Nkrumah, the charismatic head of state, and his lavish schemes for the fledgling republic.

Modernist silhouettes, such as the triumphal arch over Independence Square and the Accra Conference Centre, with its echoes of Le Corbusier's famous design for Notre Dame du Haut at Ronchamp, began to sprout on the capital's skyline. The prices of gold and cocoa, the country's main exports, soared on the world market.

Ghana's example would inspire peaceful revolution across Africa, according to Nkrumah. The colonial oppressors would be thrown off the continent. A union of independent nations would rise in their place. Yet for all his ambition, Nkrumah's plans didn't take long to unravel. The grand building projects drained the national coffers. Foreign aid dried up. The international price of cocoa fell by 60 per cent. Inflation mounted. Political unrest grew.

On 24 February 1966, while Nkrumah was on a state visit to Hanoi, the army seized power and imposed martial rule over Ghana. For the next thirteen years, military and civilian governments chased each other in and out of power. In 1979, Jerry Rawlings, a 32-year-old air force flight lieutenant, mounted a decisive coup, holding autocratic power for thirteen years before serving as elected president for a further eight years. In 2000, he was defeated in democratic elections by John Kuffour, the current president. So far, Ghana had managed four military governments and four democratic republics in the course of forty years.

It was hardly a great record. All the same, the days of political unrest were over and, from the guide book, I realized that I could retrace the country's route to independence in three stops, by walking from central Accra to Christianborg Castle on the coast, then to Independence Square.

My starting point was 28th February Road, the place where modern Ghana began. On that date in 1948, British soldiers opened fire on civil rights protesters marching along this road to the governor's residence at Christianborg Castle. Three protesters were shot dead. In the rioting that followed twelve others died. The bloodshed spurred the creation of a mass independence movement led by Nkrumah. After nine years of unrest, Britain was forced to surrender its most profitable colony in Africa to Africans themselves.

Unfortunately my walk failed to recapture those turbulent days. Twenty-Eighth February Road had become a long strip of government offices with titles such as the Office of the Public Service Commission and the Human Resources Development and Management Directorate.

Nor did matters improve when I arrived at Christianborg. The castle had served time as a Dutch trading port, the British governor's residence, a constabulary mess and a lunatic asylum, before now becoming the official seat of the Ghanaian government.

As I approached, I saw that the gates and windows were occupied by soldiers carrying submachine guns. They looked disturbingly hostile. Even the castle's ornamental gardens were posted with fearsome warnings against loitering. I stood beneath a palm tree gazing up at the castle walls, uncertain if I was banned from approaching any closer. There was no one else around, apart from a goat nibbling at the lawn beneath a 'Keep off the Grass' sign. A sinister impression crept over me that I was being watched from one of the windows. The feeling was so acute that I hurried away without looking back, only to find further disappointment at Independence Square. An amphitheatre designed to hold 30,000 people, the square probably had an amazing atmosphere when it was full. Unfortunately, with the exception of a family of chickens pecking at the ground, it was deserted when I arrived. It was as if the real Accra had taken the day off, leaving me to wander around the empty city by myself.

I sat down in the empty bleachers, exhausted by the morning's defeats. A cyclist rode across the square, the squeaking of his bicycle's wheels hovering in the air as he shrank to nothingness on the other side. Watching him labour past, it came to me that I'd been here before. On that occasion it had been night, the square filled with thousands of people celebrating Independence Day. The scent of plantain cooking on a brazier drifted over the crowd. I clung to my father's hand while the grown-ups surged around me. A troupe of stilt walkers in pierrot costumes strode past. The last of them leaned towards me. His cheeks were greasy with rouge. I smelled spirits on his breath. Wriggling free of my father in fright I burrowed into the crowd. The smell of beer and sweat surrounded me. My father grabbed my hand. He held on to me while the crowd buffeted us. What was I scared of? Looking back, it must have seemed that something malign lay behind the smeared cheeks of the pierrot. Maybe what I glimpsed in his face, and the musk of the crowd, was the sensuality of the adult world. Its normal appetites, such as alcohol and play, made grotesque by their novelty to me.

Urged on by a circle of spectators one of the pierrots was attempting a cossack dance. The crowd clapped in time, and he whirled faster and faster until he tumbled to the ground to wild cheers. My father tugged at my hand. We pushed our way out of the crowd hopping over puddles of beer. Fireworks burst overhead. I turned back and watched them dissolve into the night like exhausted stars.

From the square now, I drifted along a path running parallel to a scrappy strip of beach. A sprawling game of football was taking place. Every few minutes another passer-by kicked off his shoes and joined the match until the players resembled a shoal of fish turning through the water. Grains of sand hung in the air suspended by the sea's breeze. I watched the footballers chase the ball into the haze and transform into shadows, before cantering back into view glistening with sweat and ocean spray.

Accompanied by the murmuring of the sea I followed the path to the National Cultural Centre, a market filled with dealers selling embroidered cloths, painted face masks and ebony carvings. Among the stalls, I started searching for one of the hand-painted signs carried by itinerant barbers. The signs showed portraits of young men sporting the latest haircuts. For dramatic effect, these were normally named after a 1980s action movie such as *Top Gun* or *Rambo*. The pictures themselves always featured young men with the kind of angular high-top hairstyles favoured by American rappers fifteen years ago, as if the barbers' aesthetic universe had achieved perfection in the year 1987. It was for this reason, and not despite it, that I liked the signs and wanted to buy one. But there was confusion among the dealers when I raised the subject.

'You want haircut?' they said. 'This is craft market. You like statue. Nice statue. Good price.'

After searching to the very back of the market in case I came across an overlooked cache of the signs, I accepted another failure for the day. I'd had enough of walking around in the heat anyway.

A row of trees stood near the entrance to the market, beneath which a flock of young men had gathered, taking advantage of the shade. Each time a tourist arrived they'd swoop upon them as if with a flurry of wings and offer to guide them through the market. Only one or two would be hired. The others would return to the trees and continue scanning the horizon for fresh pickings.

I found a space beside them and leaned against a tree. As I did so a minibus rumbled to a stop at the market entrance. The guides cawed with excitement.

'What's going on?' I asked the young man next to me. Like the rest of them he was wearing a baseball cap and a basketball vest. His was yellow and purple. It said 'LA Lakers' on the front and 'Bryant' on the back.

'It's a whole bus. There are enough tourists on board for us all to get work,' he said.

The bus door opened with a sigh of hydraulics. The first tourist stepped out. He was black, with a shaven head and a white beard. He wore a dashiki and loose trousers in Ghanaian Kente weave. In his right hand he held a carved wooden staff. He set his legs wide, planted the staff in the dusty earth and looked about him, a prophet taking in his first sight of the holy land. The other passengers joined him. They wore the same printed smocks and pious expression. The guides began muttering. One of them spat resentfully on the ground.

'What's the matter?' I asked the one in the LA Lakers top.

'These people are no good,' he said. 'These are black Americans. Last year I got work as a guide with some people like this, through my uncle. He runs tours. We drove them all around Ghana for two weeks. At the start I thought they were fine people. They said to me, "We are Africans who live in America. You and us, we are the same people." We took them to the slave fort at Elmina. They all cried when they saw the dungeons. They poured a libation for the souls of their ancestors. But after a while I saw it was all words to them. Each night they stayed in a good hotel. When the food did not come fast they complained. When there was no ice in the water they complained. When the air conditioning broke down they complained. After a while all they did was complain. And they acted so high and proud as if we were their servants and they were the real Africans.'

'Not all African-Americans are like that,' I said. 'Maybe it was just the ones you were with.'

He shrugged.

'Everyone here has a similar experience. Even when we take them round the market they think they know Africa better than us.'

'So what will you do?'

He shrugged again.

'Do? We'll still guide them. Maybe we make friends with them. Maybe we get a visa to USA from them.'

I looked at the guides in their basketball vests and Nike sneakers. America for them meant Kobe and Shaq and Michael Jordan. Across from them stood the tourists. In their eyes Africa was a land of enduring wisdoms. They were its lost kings and its Nubian princesses. Both groups saw in the other a reflection of their own dreams. Africa and America converged in the car park, each searching the other's eyes for a glimpse of jungle or glittering skyscraper.

IV

When I lived in Ghana as a child I had a tortoise called Ricky. He was a lugubrious creature. Hardly the life of the party. But I liked the way he'd push out his neck and, blinking slowly, snap at the spinach leaves that I fed him. Ricky had long legs that he'd hoist up his shell on, before scuttling into the high grass behind our house.

I found him on a trail back there one day. He must have

been sleeping when they attacked. Columns of ants were streaming from the sockets of his shell. Each insect carried a diamond of flesh in their jaws. They had killed him. Now they were dismembering him from the inside.

I dug a hole with my hands in the dry red earth beside our house. There were still ants clinging to Ricky as I laid him in the grave. They ran up the outside of his shell on to my hands. One of them bit me on the fingertip. I squeezed it in half at the thorax. Then I poured the soil over Ricky until it made a soft mound over him and he was safe for ever from the ants.

That's how it was in Ghana. You never knew what shape your enemies would take.

When I first arrived at the age of two, the country seemed like a land of giants. Men walked with their bellies thrust in front of them like bull seals. The women at the market, their enormous buttocks wrapped within yards of cloth, would sit behind tubers of yam, pyramids of aubergines and trays of giant snails, fleshy and dimpled as cow tongues. But I soon found out that the scariest creatures were the smallest.

From Block O my family moved to a bungalow in Legon, a suburb of Accra. The nearest neighbour was barely within sight above the scrubland grass. In the evening my mother, who'd been raised at a convent school, sat on the porch singing 'There Is a Green Hill Far Away', 'Abide with Me' and the other melancholy hymns she associated with a happy childhood.

The ants had their home in the scrubland. From the red

earth they built fortresses that reached ten feet into the air and were impervious to anything short of heavy armaments. Within days of our arrival columns of ants marched through the kitchen and colonized the house. First they confined themselves to the food in the bin. Then they grew bolder. At breakfast they'd pick over the table for crumbs and other leavings. The dinner guest who paused with raised fork to deliver some telling bon mot would look down to find them crawling through his jollof rice. They even prised a way into the fridge. I dreaded opening the door for fear that I'd find them paddling in the juice of a mango, mandibles viscid with syrup.

Ricky was just one of their conquests. On the trails through the scrubland I'd often come across a horde of them wrestling with a butterfly or a giant beetle. They'd be trying to find a way into its exoskeleton to bite it to death. Even before the battle was over, they'd already be dragging it back to their castle.

Despite what they'd done to Ricky I didn't hate the ants. Hate I reserved for the mosquitoes.

At sunset clouds of them rose into the orange sky. Everybody was bitten. We slapped at them on the porch when they crept up our legs. We pulled the sheets over our heads in bed when we heard the outboard motor of their wings. We locked the windows and slammed the screen doors behind us to keep them out. But everybody was still bitten. And everybody got sick. It happened to me when I was four.

Lying in bed one night I noticed the temperature in

the room rising. I felt my bones twist as if they were being wound by a ratchet. The pain made me gasp. But my throat was too parched from the heat to call my parents. They found me in the morning writhing in the sheets. My mother looked into my bloodshot eyes and diagnosed malaria. They took me to Legon General Hospital. I was put to bed in a ward full of groaning children. The nurse pushed a needle into my forearm and connected a glucose drip to it. Blood blossomed, dissolving to pink in the drip tube. I felt myself drift to the ceiling, as boneless and languid as a jellyfish. When I looked down I noticed my parents had come in to sit beside the bed. Something about the intimacy with which they sat holding hands in silence made me think of them for the first time as a man and woman in their own right, not just my father and mother.

Whenever I've thought of that moment since, I can't help imagining their lives as children, too. I see my father, Joe, at the same age that I was when I fell sick, four years old.

It was 1942.

He was living in Cape Coast.

It was the year his mother died of meningitis.

With her passing, Joe and Lily, his older sister, were raised by their great-grandmother, to whom he was devoted. He slept on the floor next to her bed, looking up at the evening light as it percolated pink and green and cobalt blue though the miniature bottles of perfume on the window ledge.

Lily was fourteen years old when she came home from

school complaining she felt sick. Joe watched his great-grandmother take her to hospital. He was there as the doctors scratched their heads and said they couldn't find anything wrong with her. The family took Lily to a traditional healer who dosed her with bitter herbs. She continued to weaken. More quickly than seemed feasible, Lily was dead.

Two months later, Joe's great-grandmother was gone, too. The family said her heart was broken after Lily's death. All Joe knew was the certainty of his loneliness. At her funeral, a grown-up held him back when the cortège left to bury the coffin.

'Cemeteries are no place for young boys,' he said. Joe did as he was told. He returned to the deserted house and waited for the adults to return. He never found out where she was laid to rest.

After the funeral, Joe went to stay with his father, Joseph Eshun, the master of Zion School. He watched Joseph step out to the dances at Cape Coast Town Hall in his coat-tails and bow tie, his shoes glinting and the scent of pomade in his hair. He came to acquire some of his father's fastidiousness. At sixteen he'd have his suits hand-made by Kobena the tailor in Kotokuraba, and he spent his evenings lounging outside the Happy Bar by London Bridge, listening to Lord Kitchener's 'Trouble in Arima' and the other Trinidadian calypso records shipped over that month from Port of Spain.

The same year, 1955, he left school to work as a clerk at the United Africa Company commercial house, its ground floor piled with bolts of linen and silk, delivery boys running back and forth, and the market women cursing at the salesmen that they'd been robbed, and swearing never to return, only to come back the following week to repeat the same performance.

Now that he was a working man, Joe began courting Adelaide Newton, who lived round the corner from him on Coronation Street in a grand, four-storey house called West de Graft Hall. Adelaide would sneak out of the house to meet him. They'd watch musicals and Westerns at the Cape Coast cinema or just hang out at the Happy Bar with Joe's friends.

At the start of 1958, Adelaide discovered she was pregnant. It was the year after independence – a time of new beginnings for the country. Nkrumah had a saying to describe the infant strides of the new republic: 'Ghana, one step forward, two steps back.' With similar trepidation, my parents found themselves with a daughter to care for. They named her Araba Foriwa.

Adelaide started training to be a teacher, and Joe went to work for the Trades Union Congress (TUC) in Accra. He mixed with the activists and politicians of the new independence era. All of them believed in the promise of a free Africa. At Nkrumah's All-African People's Conference, delegates arrived from across the continent: Kenneth Kaunda of Zambia, the Kenyan trade union leader Tom Mboya, Joshua Nkomo and Robert Mugabe of Rhodesia – the young activists who'd become Africa's first generation of black leaders.

The TUC sent Joe on a nine-month scholarship to Germany, where he toured the factories and Bierkellers of Hamburg, Düsseldorf and Hanover. In the summer of 1961 he crossed Checkpoint Charlie and visited the blasted streets of East Berlin. He was still in the city when the East Germans start uncoiling barbed wire across the centre and began to erect the Wall.

From Germany, Nkrumah's party, the CPP, sent Joe to London to be its representative at the Ghana High Commission. He, Adelaide and Araba settled in Wembley and, if the work there was more prosaic than the building of a republic, there were occasional flashes of glamour. A photograph from 1964 shows Joe in a tailored three-piece suit at the Swan Hunter shipyard in Newcastle. Beside him stands the city's Lord Mayor, gold chain around his neck. Adelaide is in the foreground. A fur stole is draped over her shoulders, and there is a bottle of champagne in her right hand. She is about to smash the champagne against the steel hull of the SS *Benya River*, the latest addition to Ghana's merchant fleet. High up on the deck, sailors wave down to the crowd. Adelaide waves back. She lets go the silk cord. A camera bulb flashes. The bottle shatters. The *Benya River* slides out of the docks and begins its voyage to Accra. In the camera's glare my parents, the children of the young republic, appear to wear a halo of optimism.

Two years after the photograph was taken, however, on 24 February 1966, Nkrumah was deposed in a military coup. As a representative of the CPP, Joe lost his job. The family had to leave its house, which was rented for it by the Ghana High Commission. To exacerbate their troubles, Adelaide was nine months pregnant with their second child.

Eleven days after the coup she gave birth to a boy, Kodwo. Joe, Adelaide and the two children moved to a new house on Ealing Road, in Wembley. Joe became the leader of the CPP abroad. Nkrumah was in exile in Guinea. Joe hoped that with enough pressure Nkrumah might still be returned to power. From a three-room office in Fleet Street, Joe set up a dissenting newsletter against the military government called *Ghana Defence*.

When J. W. K. Harlley, one of the instigators of the coup, arrived in London, it was Joe who leaped on his car, causing Harlley to dive to the floor in fear of an assassination attempt.

In 1967, Joe and Adelaide had their third child, Esi. Towards the end of the same year, he told Adelaide he needed to fly to Benin for a meeting.

'I'll be back in a week,' he said.

On the day of his departure, he kissed her and each of the children, and hurried to Heathrow to catch his flight. The plane landed in Cotonou with Joe aboard. After that there was no sign of him. He'd vanished, leaving no sign of his whereabouts in Cotonou or in London.

'He's dead,' Adelaide told herself, not wanting to believe it even as the days following his disappearance became months.

Every night, she dreamed of the same scene from *The Spy Who Came in from the Cold*. It was the last film they'd seen together, but instead of Richard Burton's doomed scramble for the Berlin Wall it was Joe she saw shot down. She'd wake up to the clatter of gunfire, believing each time she'd seen him die for real.

To keep the family together, Adelaide found work at a sausage factory. When the stench of offal became more than she could bear, she moved to a night shift at the McVitie's biscuit factory in North Wembley and opened a children's day-care centre in her living room on Ealing Road. Eighteen-hour working days and, each time she shut her eyes, there was Joe still trying to scale the Wall.

From the beginning of his disappearance, Adelaide learned not to rely on her neighbours for help. The elderly white woman next door would ignore her even when they were both standing in their back gardens, with just a fence between them. There was the time the pipes burst, leaking through into the woman's house. The first Adelaide knew about it was when a constable arrived at her front door. Instead of calling round the woman had rung the police.

Strangers proved just as spiteful. At MacFisheries on Wembley high street, she waited her turn at the counter. Waited and waited while the white women behind her were served first. When she complained, the fishmonger affected to notice her for the first time.

'In this country,' he said, 'we prefer to queue.'

She left, trying and failing to hold back tears.

Six months after Joe vanished, a friend of his called at Ealing Road. He had a wheedling manner that made it difficult to follow his conversation. Adelaide understood from him that Joe might be alive and in Ghana.

Another four months later, she received a letter signed by Joe himself. He'd been abducted by government agents as he landed at Cotonou. For the past year, they had held him in detention at Ussher Fort in Accra. He was a political prisoner. It was only much later that Adelaide discovered that the man who'd come simpering to Ealing Road was the one who'd betrayed Joe to the government. Even with the relief of Joe's letter, there was still no way to see him. Conditions were still too volatile for her to return to Ghana.

And by then there was a fourth child to consider. Unknown to either of them when Joe left for Benin, Adelaide had been pregnant with their second son. I was born nine months afterwards, in May 1968. She named me Ekow, after Joe's Fante name.

I saw my father for the first time two years later. By then the government had conceded they had no case against him. On his release we flew to Accra to meet him. Seated on the plane, Adelaide thought about all the things she wanted to say to him about the children, and her time in London. And she found herself wondering if he might apologize for her loneliness and turbid dreams.

In the event neither of them did much talking. When he saw her, Joe began to cry. She held him as he wept, and the two of them exchanged tears in place of words, while the children clutched at their parents' legs, excited and uncertain about the meaning of the adults' behaviour.

My earliest memories belong to that day. Thinking back, I cannot recall anything of how my parents looked – only the sensation of being caught between them. The bristles of Joe's beard, the scent of Adelaide's perfume and the force of my own tears as their reunion finally came to bear.

That was how I ended up living in Ghana as a child. We arrived in 1971 and stayed for three years. Araba went to boarding school in Cape Coast. When we came to school age, Esi, Kodwo and I were enrolled at Burma Camp in Accra. Burma Camp was not very different from being drafted. The red-brick bungalows of the school were set within the grounds of Accra's main military barracks. From my classroom window I could hear a drill sergeant bawl orders to his men away across the playing fields. Burma Camp wasn't an army school; it just shared the same grounds as the barracks. But discipline was martial. Mr Frankson, my class teacher, kept a cane above the blackboard. I never saw him use it, but he was still generous in slaps applied to the backs of young heads. He was a pastor in an evangelical church and seemed to believe our class existed in a state of permanent moral emergency.

'Indiscipline is a sin,' said Mr Frankson. 'You must work to purge it from your souls.'

I'd made the mistake of giggling during one of his extemporary sermons once. He'd covered the ground quickly for a small man. Before I could compose myself, he was at the back of the room clapping me over the ear. I had to spend lunch composing an essay on the theme of

'Honour Your Elders' with a ringing head and teary eyes.

Once a week the boys in the school did drill, stamping dust beneath bare feet as we marched round the playing field. The point of this escaped me. For all the marching we always ended up where we had started. But in the physical repetition of actions – turn, march, turn, halt, march, turn, eyes right, halt, attention – my mind was at least free to follow its own course. I thought about chocolate biscuits and ice cream – luxuries almost impossible to come by in Ghana. They meant Britain to me. I knew there was something else, too, called, 'chips'. I wasn't sure whether it was hot or sweet or sharp to taste, but like chocolate biscuits and ice cream it held the promise of unqualified delight.

'Isaac Dunkor. Elizabeth Foster . . .' said Mr Frankson. He looked around the class with narrowed eyes. Then he read out the last name on his list.

'Ekow Eshun.'

Mr Frankson led the three of us out of the classroom and along the silent corridors, until we reached a storeroom normally used for buckets and mops. He opened the door. It was the size of a closet. There were five children already in there. By the light of the corridor I made out Esi and Kodwo. Mr Frankson stood over us in the doorway. 'Wo ye nyimpa bon,' he said. 'You are bad children. You must stay in here the rest of the afternoon. We will call your parents and they can come and get you. Until then I don't want to see you.'

He shut the door and left us in the dark.

Elizabeth Foster started to cry. I felt like crying, too. What had we done that was so criminal apart from turn up for school that morning?

'We haven't done anything wrong,' said Esi, reading my mind. 'I heard some of the teachers talking yesterday about parents who hadn't paid their fees yet. They said that if the school didn't get its fees, then they wouldn't get their wages. So something had to be done about it. I think this is what they decided to do.'

We started discussing whether it was true or not. Then the talking subsided. Whatever the reason, we were shut in a dark room smelling of ammonia for the afternoon. We tried to get comfortable, but there wasn't enough space for us all to sit on the floor. I stood between two mops and shut my eyes. If I tried to blank out the room and the school and the whole of Ghana then, when I opened my eyes, I might be back in Britain, and there'd be all the chips and ice cream I could eat. I squeezed my eyes shut until I could see the red behind my eyelids. I took a gulp of air and held my breath. Blood thrummed in my ears. My fingers gripped my shoulders. Nails dug into skin. I couldn't hold on any longer. My eyes were opening. I was breathing again. And I was still in the same room. Elizabeth Foster was still crying. It still stank of ammonia. I started crying, too.

Some time later the door opened. It was Mr Frankson. And behind him my mother. She looked angry. He looked embarrassed. I wondered what she'd said to him. But the lump in my throat was too big to say anything. I took her hand. She smothered my head at her waist. Esi and Kodwo and I followed her out of school, walking quickly. It was still light outside. She was very quiet and so were we. That evening after dinner, without a word of explanation, she served us each a bowl of vanilla ice cream.

The idea was to return home.

In 1974, General Ignatius Acheampong stared from the television screen announcing that he'd led the army in an overthrow of the government. My family made plans to leave the country. My father had secured another posting to the Ghana High Commission in London. The idea was that by spending his four-year term abroad we could sidestep the worst of the turmoil before returning to Ghana. Despite the upheavals they'd already faced, it didn't occur to my parents that something might disrupt their plan.

For years afterwards in Britain they pored over blueprints of house designs, drawn out on crackly translucent paper, trying to decide which style of house to build once we went back to Accra. In the garage my mum kept two metal shipping trunks that each month grew more full with Moulinex food blenders, Marks & Spencer towels and all the other essentials of modern family living.

A temporary stopover, then. But what does five-year-old Ekow think of the plan in Accra? Concupiscent fantasies fill his head. His belly swells in anticipation of the chips and ice cream and chocolate biscuits about to come its way. Those are *his* plans. That's what home means to him. Not Block O or the dimly remembered greyness of London, but the satiation of desire.

So, eagerly, we board the Ghana Airways plane. Knowing we'll be back soon, Joe and Adelaide leave Araba at boarding school in Cape Coast. Kodwo, Esi and I are shepherded up the stairs. All of us, as we turn for a last look at the control tower and the city beyond it, believe in the beneficence of the future. We believe it will deliver us home. All of us suspect nothing of what lies ahead.

Two steps forward, one step back.

The future, it turns out, isn't all ice cream.

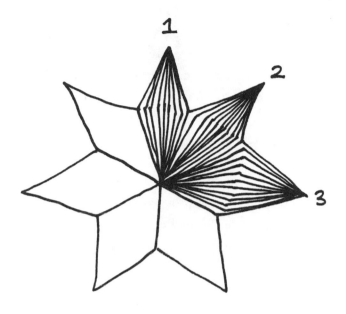

*The exoticism of suburbia – My racist friends – Watching
the black-and-white minstrels – Jerry Rawlings's coup –
The vanishings – Kodwo as Reed Richards – At the
Ghana High Commission*

I

It is 1976 and the famously hot summer of that year is
at its zenith. In the London suburb of Queensbury a hose-
pipe ban leaves gardens parched and golden. A music-box
rendition of 'Greensleeves' is heard at four o'clock each

afternoon to mark the arrival of the Mr Whippy van with its promise of Mivvys, Fabs and 99 Cones. And at number 176 Beverly Drive the Eshuns are planning a party.

The Jubilee Line has recently opened and if you run your finger north on a tube map, past the vale of blighted names that is Kilburn, Willesden and Neasden, you will come eventually to Queensbury, where my family has lived for the past year.

We arrived after a prolonged tour of northwest London. There was the cramped flat in Willesden where we first decamped from the Ghana Airways plane and sat in a daze watching television as Franz Beckenbauer scored for West Germany against Holland in the 1974 World Cup final. From Willesden we moved to a shrunken terraced house in Wembley that proved unpopular with my siblings and me as soon as we stepped inside and learned all three of us had to share a room. As I lay listening to them breathe at night I would think of how you could run and run through the scrubland behind our house in Legon, the long grass whipping at your face, without ever bumping into another human being. When you stopped you heard the beetles scratching through the undergrowth. Greenbottles buzzed in your ear. Butterflies wove erratic patterns among the wild flowers.

Even by yourself, you were never alone in Ghana. It was different in London. The houses of Wembley were made of red brick, and they were forced together in narrow streets. There were lots of people around, wheeling babies in pushchairs and hefting bags of food home from the shops. But for all the activity, I couldn't get over how quiet it seemed. In Ghana, a child tripping over or any other minor incident would draw a crowd of onlookers offering contradictory advice vastly out of proportion to the incident itself. *They*, not the child nursing a grazed knee, were the true centre of the drama. Without them, London seemed empty of life.

After Wembley we moved to the house in Queensbury where we now lived. Crazy paving was the dominant feature of the driveways here. Each Sunday, Ford Cortinas and Vauxhall Cavaliers were washed and polished with religious devotion. Our house had pebble-dashed walls and a conservatory at the back with Velux windows. An apple tree and a pear tree stood within an expanse of back garden. At exactly 6.15 each evening a police constable strolled past the front gate. We waved at him and he raised a hand to the brim of his helmet in return. Harold Trescothick, the old man who lived alone next door, would sometimes invite me in to share a bag of chips and leaf through his collection of stamps from Tallinn, Lima, Newfoundland and lots of other cities with which I was less than familiar. Moving to Queensbury was like waking up to find yourself in the pages of a Ladybird book with its watercolour illustrations of life in Britain. Here was somewhere truly exotic.

It was the summer holidays and in the back garden Esi sat with her back to the apple tree unfolding the three-page image of Elizabeth Taylor's arrival in Rome as Cleopatra from the *Encyclopaedia of Epic Films*. Beside her, Kodwo was describing Shelob's lair in *The Return of the King*, with close attention to the grimmer details of how the giant spider ingested its prey. Taller, smarter and two years older than me, Kodwo was the family's presiding genius. At ten, he had long, tapering fingers and an imperious manner that left me feeling like a melted candle beside him. Instead of joining their conversation I practised handstands on the dried-out lawn.

Balanced upside-down, my mind turned to a school trip the previous month to the Museum of London. My class had gone to see an exhibition on the Great Fire of London. For days beforehand, I lay awake picturing the scenes of spectacular destruction it promised. Yet as we crossed the overpass leading into the museum I stood frozen in place while the class streamed past me.

Silently, as it appeared from behind the glass of the overpass, I saw my father's midnight-blue Volvo estate pass by underneath. Through the windscreen I had a clear view of the curve of his forehead. The sun glinted from his glasses. Mr Johnson, his chauffeur, sat beside him in a grey suit, his hands wrapped in brown leather gloves working the wheel. My father leaned towards him and mouthed an instruction. Clouds rippled on the car's metal skin. It swept beneath the bridge towards St Paul's.

When he asked me about the school trip that evening I didn't tell my dad about the overpass. Spotting him had felt like gazing down into the secret workings of the adult world. I didn't want anything to damage that impression, not even his consciousness of it.

Every morning Mr Johnson collected my father for work in the Volvo, the car drawing up in front of the house powerful as a dray horse. Fixed to its grille was a diplomatic plate, meaning that, as sovereign Ghanaian territory, the Volvo could speed through red lights, park on double yellow lines or race down the corridors of Buckingham Palace with total impunity, or at worst the risk of a mild international incident.

After he came home in the evening, my father would shave standing at the bathroom mirror, then come downstairs, the natural force of him, his solemnity, the volume of his breathing, filling the living room. When I was very young I used to climb over him while he watched television, as if he were a mountain range. I'd haul myself up the rock face of his legs, then sprawl on the plateau of his stomach, its churnings seismic in their mystery below me.

In those days I could imagine my father only from the outside. What I've learned since of his vulnerability and his sadness have tempered that impression. But nothing can erase the memory of looking up at him as a child to find him staring back, as if he were peering down through the clouds.

On the Saturday of the party, my dad slid open the patio doors and dragged the wooden speaker boxes of his quadraphonic stereo on to the lawn. From the attic he hauled down the boxes of Chivas Regal and Johnny Walker Black

Label that he'd buy duty-free on the return leg of a diplomatic mission. In the kitchen, chicken legs spattered in the frying pan. My mother set a huge saucepan of jollof rice on the cooker to simmer. Loaves of kenkey wrapped in banana leaves sat in a pile, stinking of entropy.

As the doorbell chimed and the guests began arriving I watched two worlds coalesce. The adults came dressed in Kente cloth robes flung over bare shoulders. On their feet they wore *mpagoa*, leather sandals in emerald and gold. The women had jewelled fingers and elaborately constructed headscarves. They had grown up in the same sprawling households back in Ghana and called each other brother and sister. There were Mr Campbell Rhodes, a friend of my father's, an enormous man always dressed in a tight-fitting sky-blue safari suit that seemed in danger of imminent rupture; Auntie Christina from Cricklewood, a martyr to her teeth ever since an unscrupulous dentist had whipped out her entire upper set during a routine check-up; my mother's sister Panyin, who had a twin called Kakra, their names in Fante meaning 'Older' and 'Younger'. There were diplomats, pastors, the wife of a former vice president, the daughter of a popular highlife singer, the boss of a thriving goat-meat concern and innumerable others whose names have blurred now, but were revealed that night to be fabulous dancers, dazzling storytellers or evil drunks.

Beneath the apple tree at the end of the garden, Esi, Kodwo and I were gathered with their sons and daughters. From Nottingham, our cousins Charles, Albert and

Betsey, the boys in matching blue suits made by their mother; Penelope and Eurydice, the heavenly sisters from Twickenham upon whom I maintained a silent and wholly unrequited crush; Ezra and Ezekiel, who lived in Luton and wore about them a morbid air that surely came from bearing names hewn from the dark matter of the Old Testament. From Brooklyn came my teenage cousin Marcus, sent to London for the summer by my mother's sister in New York, after he'd taken to running with a wild crowd in Flatbush. Marcus wore a gold chain round his neck and spoke in a confidential drawl that forced us all to cluster round him.

'Back home, I got a gun, yo. But I let one of my boys carry it so I don't get caught with a piece.'

'Wowww,' we all said.

'Shit is crazy hectic out there sometimes, yo. Dude gotta pack *something*,' said Marcus. 'Yo, y'all know how it is, right?'

We nodded vigorously, although I doubt any of us had any idea about how 'it' was.

However tenuously we were related, us kids formed a family for that night. From the end of the garden we watched as our parents danced to the Mighty Sparrow. Our mothers waved handkerchiefs above their heads and twirled in circles, their steps precise within tight skirts. Fathers did the shimmy and the side-to-side slide, summoning the dance steps of their youth with varying degrees of success. As we watched, my dad patted the air with his hands for quiet. The grown-ups formed a semicircle round him.

He raised an open bottle of gin and recited a remembrance in Fante to family, forebears and Ghana. The adults bowed their heads. Gin splashed on the grass. At the back of the garden Kodwo rolled his eyes and gave a theatrical yawn. The pouring of a libation occurred at every family gathering. It was always greeted with derision by the younger generation.

'Why can't they just let the music play?' said Kodwo, trying to swing from the lowest branch of the apple tree.

How much of that scorn was envy, I wonder now? Our parents had their rituals and dance steps. They knew where they were from. By contrast all that connected us was distance from Ghana. Born in Britain, it seemed to us that we were the adults. We bore the pressure of growing up in a strange country while our parents played on the grass like children.

II

Some of my best friends were racists.

At Queensbury Junior School there were no African children apart from the Eshuns. So far I'd failed to turn up with a bone through my nose, but collective wisdom among the members of Class 3B held Africa to be a place of mud huts and cannibals. This from the same kids who conducted earnest debates on the best way to light farts and flick bogeys.

To Greg O'Rourke, the aggressively freckled Jamie

Brown, Benny Mitchell with his lazy eye and the rest of 3B, England was an amalgam of Arthurian lore and Dunkirk spirit, predicated on the dominance of the white race over wogs, Pakis and Yids. In the playground they spread their arms wide like Spitfires, ack-acking at the Hun while they chorused the theme tune to *The Dam Busters*. It was their innocence that appalled me most. These were chubby-legged boys who burped like frogs over lunch. What did they know about giant snails or ants that could kill a tortoise? What did they know about Burma Camp?

And if they didn't know, how could I begin to tell them? When my mind drifted off in the playground, I pictured beggars with rickets and kids my age with the swollen bellies that came from drinking contaminated water. I remembered General Acheampong's face on television, gleaming with sweat. So I said nothing. And they drew their own conclusions about me.

I seemed to elicit a fascination in them. They patted my hair for springiness and pulled the coils straight to test its tensile strength. In the sunshine of an outdoor swimming lesson the water shone iridescent on my skin. Sage words were exchanged on its seal-like consistency, and fingers pinched at my arms to see if I carried an extra layer of fat. Only my eyes and teeth would be visible in the dark they insisted, reaching for the light switch to test their theories.

Eyes moist with compassion, Mrs O'Rourke bent towards me outside the school gates. 'And what tribe are you from, dear?'

'I live on Beverly Drive, Mrs O'Rourke.'
'Yes, dear, but where are you *really* from?'

I couldn't blame them. My friends grew up on Tarzan movies and TV series about white heroes in the bush such as *Daktari* and *Cowboy in Africa*. Everywhere they looked black people stood dumb and bestial. All they had to do was open the *Beano* to find the piccaninny girl in *Lord Snooty* with her big, white eyes and knotted hair. In *Doctor Doolittle*, the 'mud-coloured' Prince Bumpo offered half his kingdom to the good doctor in exchange for being turned white. A jungle tribe worshipped wooden statues of Tintin and Snowy in *Tintin in the Congo*.

The closer you looked, the worse it got. At peak time on Saturday nights, BBC One would broadcast the *Black & White Minstrel Show*. It wasn't a programme my family made an effort to watch. Sometimes I'd catch it while alone in the living room, though, and I'd sit mesmerized as the minstrels smacked their lips and plucked their banjos. It took me a while to realize the show was set in a skewed version of the antebellum South. Eyes rolling like marbles it seemed they couldn't have been happier than when they leaned their heads together for a close harmony rendition of 'Ol' Man River'.

As the cameras drew tighter I saw their faces glistening with greasepaint under the studio lights. Pink tongues flickered in white-rimmed mouths. Beneath the mask of black imbecility another consciousness stirred. What did the world look like through the eyes of a Black and White

Minstrel? At its peak the programme drew 16 million viewers. When it was cancelled in 1978, there were letters of protest to the BBC and revivals that toured for years after on the regional stage. George Mitchell, the show's creator, always insisted it was harmless entertainment. But remembering what I glimpsed in the faces of his minstrels I'm not so sure. Behind the make-up, their eyes flashed with an awareness of their real mission. This, I believe, was to occlude the difference between the fantasy and reality of black people. The minstrels weren't truly pretending to be black. Their job was to reflect how a white audience wanted to see blacks: as supine, childlike and cretinous. The same way we were presented, with less sophistication, in *Tintin*, *Tarzan* and *Lord Snooty*.

Cloaked as entertainment the programme was ostensibly victimless. At school the following Monday, when Mr Ramsden the PE teacher liked to tell me I had a chip on my shoulder, I could see its consequences. Unless I was as quiescent as a Black and White Minstrel I deserved to be cautioned and, in Mr Ramsden's case, given detention for 'too much lip'. Fantasy was as potent as reality.

Over on ITV you could find *Love Thy Neighbour*, a sitcom about a Caribbean couple who moved next door to a white racist and his wife. It was supposed to show prejudice as farce by revealing both men as bigots who traded insults across the garden fence.

'Sambo.'

'Honky.'

'Nig-nog.'

'Whitey.'

To my ears, the white barbs dug deeper than the black ones. Any time I watched the show, I could feel my skin prickle.

'Coon. Monkey. Wog. Jungle bunny. Rubber lips. With your smelly food and your jungle drums. Taking our jobs. Go back to where you come from.'

The audience laughed and laughed, but I could never see what was funny. Or for that matter what was amusing about *Rings on their Fingers*, *Mind Your Language*, *Till Death Us Do Part* and the other comedies based on the notion that black people were as entertaining as chimps in the zoo.

From what I could make out race was the great obsession of 1970s Britain. When Cyrille Regis, Laurie Cunningham and Brendan Batson signed for West Bromwich Albion, the crowd hurled bananas at them. If one of these players came near the touchline the fans dropped the fruit and spat instead.

On August Bank Holiday, Kodwo, Esi and I would watch TV news reports of the Notting Hill Carnival, howling at the screen. It was the same every year. First a grave-voiced announcement about the number of arrests that year, as if the festival was nothing but a face-off between the police and black youth. Then images of policemen dancing in the street with an overweight black woman. Threat followed by passivity. Black people might seem frightening, but at heart they were really happy children.

'They could at least vary it one year,' said Kodwo, after

we'd turned off the screen in disgust. 'Like they could arrest some fat women or something, or ban pictures of police posing with coconuts as fake breasts.'

Did white people act as they did out of ignorance or malice? It was hard to say, but the question seemed to be getting more urgent. Eyebrows knitted, Mrs Thatcher worried that Britain was in danger of being 'swamped' by 'people with a different culture'. The British Movement was marching on Brick Lane, and bands with skinhead fans such as Sham 69 and Cockney Rejects were playing *Top of the Pops*.

A fashion for fourteen-hole Doc Marten boots swept the third year of Queensbury Juniors. Kids essayed furtive 'Sieg heils' when teachers turned their backs. They chalked 'Wogs out' on the playground walls and carved National Front logos in the desks with their compasses.

Leaving assembly I accidentally knocked into Kevin Dyer. As I stepped back he flung a punch at my head. My glasses spun to the floor. Blinking, I saw him crouched before me, fists balled. A crowd of boys formed round us. 'Cunt,' he said, pale eyes bulging.

'Blackcunt.'

'Fuckingblackcunt.'

Hands shoved me towards him.

Voices hissed in my ear.

'You're not going to let him get away with that, are you?'

I clenched my fists and set my legs apart. Kevin Dyer snarled at me.

'Come on then, you cunt,' he said.

I wanted to hit him. I could feel my fist dent into his cheek until it met the resistance of bone. I wanted his lips bloody and his eyes swollen shut. But even as I imagined this I watched myself break free of the circle of boys and pick up my glasses.

'He's bottled it,' said a voice behind me, as I walked away.

Why didn't I stay? Was I too scared to stand up for myself? It was true I felt shaken. But the sensation of fear was missing when I turned away. Even anger had drained away. I was quite calm.

What did it matter what Kevin Dyer called me? If I went looking I could find the words 'black cunt' scratched into a desk just as easily as hear it from his lips.

'Wog', 'rubber lips', 'sambo', 'jungle bunny' – the words drifted through the school like background radiation. You just had to stand in the corridor as the kids rushed between classes and your Geiger counter would start clicking like crazy. In school, on television, out in the street, they were completely commonplace.

Every time I heard them they still hurt, though. I told myself they described me no better than the glistening face of a black-and-white minstrel. In doing so, I realized I faced a choice between fantasy and truth. Either I could play along with white people's expectations of me as a minstrel or I could confound their prejudice and seek out the real, paradoxical nature of the world. That was the true fight. What did Kevin Dyer matter by comparison?

III

On 4 June 1979 my childhood ended.

I'd just turned eleven. Family photos show me poised with a spoon, about to rain destruction on a chocolate fudge sundae at Baskin Robbins during birthday celebrations. Benny Mitchell, Greg O'Rourke, Jamie Brown and I had just watched *Battlestar Galactica* at the Empire cinema, Leicester Square, in 'Sensurround'. In our violently stimulated state, laser blasts seemed to caroom round the white-tiled walls of the ice-cream parlour. As I pictured it at that moment the future involved screaming guns and faster-than-light star cruisers.

After my birthday, though, the green leather family photo albums that had recorded first days at school in awkward new uniforms, outings to Hampton Court and grumbling visits to obscure relatives go blank. The Eshuns turn away from the camera. Our attention is diverted by foreign affairs. On 4 June a coup takes place in Ghana. The photo albums are a void after this date because, for us, the promise of a vivid future has become a thing of the past.

In the beginning the word meant nothing to me. I heard it repeated over and over behind the door of the living room as aunties and uncles huddled in conference with my parents. From their hushed tones it was obviously something fearful.

'Two steps forward, one step back,' I heard my mother say, to murmured agreement.

But how bad could a 'coup' be?

As far as I could tell from eavesdropping, the grown-ups were debating whether to stay in London or return to Ghana. That would mean enrolment at Mfanstipim, Achimota or one of the country's other boarding schools where the boys slept in dorm rooms, wore shorts till they were sixteen and saluted in the presence of teachers. It was not a prospect I looked forward to.

In the *Observer* that Sunday I saw for the first time a picture of Flight Lieutenant Jerry Rawlings. He was tall and light-skinned, the child of a Ghanaian mother and a Scottish father. The coup had been staged by junior ranking officers like him from their base at Burma Camp. Rawlings called it a revolution. Politicians and senior army officers of the previous regime were being arrested en masse, said the report. Afrifra, Acheampong and Akuffo, the three former heads of state, were to stand trial on corruption charges under penalty of death. I read through the story a second time and put the newspaper down.

Judging by the reaction of the grown-ups, the coup was a grave event. To me it sounded thrilling. I pictured crowds amok on the streets of Accra. The mighty being torn from their palaces. Buccaneers seizing the crown. It was like a real-life version of *The Count of Monte Cristo* or *The Prince and the Pauper*.

No one had asked my opinion about returning to Ghana – I was against it for reasons of tight discipline and dorm rooms – but a febrile atmosphere pervaded the house. There were late-night crisis meetings, phone calls from Accra at unfeasible hours, aunties in tears on the doorstep. If a coup meant the upending of the existing order, then it was already working its magic. One step forward, two steps back. There was no way to tell where we were heading any more.

Perhaps it's because of this, because I was dazzled by the realization that the adult world was no more ordered than a child's, that I failed to notice the real effects of the coup until it was too late. I couldn't have done anything to stop them, of course. But it might have given me the chance to reflect that when it comes, change rarely takes the form you expect.

That summer my parents didn't throw a party.

In the attic the supplies of duty-free whisky and brandy ran dry. The sweep of a torch revealed only the broken Scalextric sets and radio-controlled helicopters of Christmases past. My heart still beat a secret rhythm for Penelope and Eurydice, but we hardly had any visitors to the house any more.

Yet for a while it seemed we were too far from its epicentre to feel the coup's tremors. My father disappeared into the Volvo every morning. My mother made jollof rice and chicken stew. On Sundays, Kodwo, Esi and I sprawled on their bed, eating toast and reading the newspapers, the radio tuned to the World Service for news about Ghana. From round the globe I heard reports of natural disasters and threatening noises made to the west by Mr Brezhnev. There was nothing from Ghana, though. Squashed between my parents while our neighbours washed their cars outside, it felt as if there could be no safer place on earth.

It was round then the disappearances started. I noticed it first with the wood-panelled Sony Betamax recorder. My father had heaved it home in the primitive dawn of domestic video manufacture and it had remained with us for years, defeating all attempts to make it record, until, overtaken by the march of VHS, it had been retired to an ornamental position beneath a doily in the living room. Without explanation the Betamax vanished one day, leaving behind nothing but a pale rectangle on the sideboard. Its departure was followed by the industrial-sized Nikon camera with which, crouched behind a tripod, my dad used to corral Esi, Kodwo and me into posing for him while we whinnied like foals. From the garage my mother's shipping trunks went missing. Even the signet ring my father had always worn on his left hand disappeared.

They'd made up their mind and we were going back to Ghana, I decided, ferreting through their dressing table for an Achimota school prospectus or other signs of imminent departure. For all the discomforts of school, I'd grown used to Queensbury. I knew the way through the maze of alleyways that ran behind our house and why it was a good idea to avoid the chip shop on Roe Green Lane, haunt of the neighbourhood skinheads. I liked the wild raspberries that grew in Harold Trescothick's back garden and the giant jars of acid drops and lemon sherbets arrayed behind the counter at Stanford's, the corner shop.

For a week I expected to hear that we'd be following the Betamax abroad. My parents said nothing, though. It was as if they were waiting for a sign. By Sunday, with still no word, I started to relax. Stretched out on my parents' bed reading the football scores I'd missed most of the World Service report until my father turned up the volume. Afrifra, Acheampong and Akuffo had been found guilty, said the newscaster. Their sentence would be death by firing squad. Far from bringing order to Ghana, Rawlings had proved to be just another tyrant. My mother looked at my father.

'We can't go home,' she said. 'When they start killing people this is too much.'

It may have been that they were waiting until that verdict to make up their minds. Yet somehow I doubt it. If I could have looked beyond my appetite for wild raspberries and lemon sherbets I might have realized they'd already made their decision. The possessions disappearing from our house weren't being shipped to Ghana, but jettisoned to make room for our new life.

It was only then that we began feeling the impact of the coup. As an employee of the previous regime it was too dangerous for my father to return home. But staying meant the surrender of all his official ties with Ghana. By the end of the summer there had been a new round of disappearances. This time they took place in full view. My father left his job. With it went the midnight-blue Volvo. And also our house which had been rented for us by the High Commission.

Packing the remainder of our possessions into a removal lorry we left on a brilliantly clear day, the splendour of which struck me as mocking tribute to our downfall. Harold Trescothick waved weakly from his front door, but I felt too miserable to say goodbye. Squeezed into the back of a rented Ford Escort beside Esi, Kodwo and a quantity of suitcases, I stared furiously at the frayed laces on my trainers, trying to keep my mind blank of apple trees and summer parties so I wouldn't start to cry.

Not that we were going far. Our new house stood in a row of terraces in the neighbouring suburb of Kingsbury. It had a small back garden and three bedrooms that seemed ominously cramped by the time the removal men had unpacked the lorry. The scent of perfume hovered in the bathroom. Long strands of brown hair clogged the sink. Outside a dog barked maniacally. No one tried to stop it. On foot, the distance between Kingsbury and Queensbury was only twenty minutes, but it seemed to me that we'd crossed a chasm. Perhaps all of the things that disappeared from our life still exist somewhere in the gulf, I reflected. Maybe they never went away at all. Maybe it's us that have vanished instead.

IV

Across the divide, the laws of nature were now inverted.

My father stayed home while my mother went to work. She had found a job as an auxiliary nurse on the geriatric ward of Edgware General Hospital. In the evening she'd arrive home hobbling, trailed by the scent of antiseptic. I pictured her tending to the flesh of her patients, watching some bloom and others wither. Her back ached, she said. Her face was more lined than I remembered. Broadly speaking, however, I was an unsympathetic witness to her troubles.

'Is it too much to ask?' she said. 'Can't you children clean up before I get home?'

My mum surveyed the disorder of wax crayons, odd shoes, overturned poufs and tattered *Fantastic Four* comics that Esi, Kodwo and I had wrought on the living room. We shrugged in unison and ran upstairs before she could make us tidy up.

'What's she got to complain about?' said Kodwo in the bedroom he and I shared. 'It's not as if we don't do enough round here.'

The Eshun brothers nodded in agreement. It was a moment of rare accord. Since the move we'd spent much of our time arguing.

Each of us had taken the coup as a personal tragedy. I used to get 50p-a-week pocket money in Queensbury, which I spent on the *Beano*, the *Dandy* and a quarter pound of acid drops. I had a Scalextric set, a skateboard and a complete collection of Asterix books. The Volvo sat in front of the house and the fridge was stocked with Coke and Fanta. I accepted it all without reflection. I assumed that's how you were *supposed* to live in Britain.

Kingsbury offered a different lesson. Under its inverse laws, everything that had been was no more. Apart from pocket money and Fanta, there was also the absence of electrical appliances. In place of a washing machine my mum scrubbed our clothes in the bathtub on Saturday mornings. Kodwo, Esi and I had to take over after she grew tired. When it was my turn I knelt at the edge of the tub scrubbing T-shirts, underwear and socks until my shoulders ached. If no one was looking, I turned on the hot tap, tipped the washing powder into the water and lost myself in sculpting castles and Easter Island heads out of the foam.

In recent months I had acquired an array of new skills. I could darn my socks and stitch the holes in my school jumpers. In the absence of a vacuum cleaner I knew how to sweep against the nap of a carpet with a dustpan and brush in order to work loose the grey whorls of lint. Using only the cranky manual lawn mower I could conjure an even lawn out of the unkempt back garden. I had learned how to spray the sideboards and coffee table of the front room with a can of Pledge to leave it clean and, as I was assured on the label, pine fresh.

None of these talents was a source of pride. I would sooner have been at Benny Mitchell's house making his Stunt Cycle Evel Knievel pop wheelies. Or helping Jamie

Brown build Autobots and Decepticons from his extensive collection of Transformers figures.

I collected the wet clothes from the bath, heaved them to the back garden in a basket, and started to peg them on the washing line. When I was alone I wanted to wail like a baby until someone came rushing over to tell me everything would be all right. It was an urge of almost overwhelming force.

Sometimes while I was still a toddler, I'd sit up in my bed and bang the back of my head against the wall. This is a sign of distress that I've seen subsequently on TV documentaries about abandoned infants. At the time I found it comforting. After I finished hanging up the washing I went up to my room. I sat against the wall, and bumped my head against it over and over. My hair cushioned the harshness of impact. The sensation wasn't like pain. It was as if the wall were patting my head. Each time I hit it I felt as if everything might be all right.

I hadn't cried once since we had left Queensbury. Not even on the first night, when I lay awake listening to the swish of fir trees from the neighbour's garden until the sky began to lighten. I often felt the tears gather. But I was afraid if I started to cry they might not stop. Anger felt just as dangerous. If I shouted the fragility of our new existence might collapse, leaving us with nothing at all. In place of tantrums I contrived small rebellions: a messy living room or, on the days I was consigned to washing-up duty, I'd allow a wet plate to slip through my fingers and shatter on the floor tiles with a satisfying din.

I was hollow. I was devoured by hurt.

I could see the same sadness in the rest of my family. In the evenings we sat in the living room arguing about politics, what to watch on television and anything else apart from the coup. We had been struck dumb by a combination of shame and stoicism. It was as if we each blamed ourselves for our downfall.

For every one of us there were possessions – a signet ring or an apple tree – that counted for something special. Recalling them meant acknowledging they were gone for good. So we filled the living room with conversation to avoid saying what was really on our minds. Our dream of home had come to nothing.

V

In the classic Stan Lee and Jack 'King' Kirby Marvel comics of the early 1960s, the Fantastic Four's headquarters on the thirty-fifth floor of New York's Baxter Building was home to a phantasmagoria of particle smashers and ionic triangulators, their steel flanks rendered in gleaming detail by Kirby's artwork. Because those were the comics I loved back then and because, even today, I think of Kodwo as Reed Richards, the FF's prodigiously smart leader, this is how I have come to remember the bedroom my brother and I shared in Kingsbury.

The room was filled with Marvel comics, science-fiction paperbacks and Kodwo's collection of progressive rock records – all accumulated in vast quantities that seemed to us to provide a bulwark between the outside world and our private domain. Both of us failed to anticipate the impact of the coup, however, which smashed through our defences like a boulder from a giant catapult. In the silence that overtook my family in its aftermath, the bedroom came to feel more like a war zone than a refuge. The battle that took place was internal, each of us struggling with the dislocation of moving – first from Ghana to Britain, then Queensbury to Kingsbury. Unfortunately we lacked the ability to express how we felt.

Kodwo and I shared the room all through adolescence. During that time neither of us found the words to articulate our sorrow. We settled for rivalry instead. By the time he was sixteen and I was fourteen we couldn't stand the sight of each other.

Across the room's mauve carpet, wash tides of *X-Men* and *Fantastic Four* comics swept between our beds. Crossing their surface was perilous. You could slip on the glossy cover of the *Avengers*, issue 186 ('Enter . . . Mordred the Mystic!') and find yourself pitched over into an alluvial deposit of *Spider-Mans* and *Ghost Riders*. Ankles had been twisted. Tempers risked a fraying on entry. Heedless to all potential calamity, the tide rose higher each month.

What was behind our devotion to Marvel? With hindsight I see now that the attraction of those comics didn't lie in cosmological fantasy so much as with the heroes' attempts to carve normal lives out of their extraordinary circumstances. The FF had it easy. Reed and Sue Richards, the Invisible Woman, were married. Johnny Storm, the Human Torch, was a hot-rod-driving playboy. Only Ben Grimm, the monstrous, orange-skinned Thing, was an outsider, and even his pain was soothed by the love of Alicia Masters, the blind sculptor.

With adolescence I switched allegiance to the X-Men, who lived in secrecy bedevilled by paranoias, schizophrenias and bouts of homicidal rage. In my isolation I felt a tug of empathy when I saw them spurned by the humans they'd pledged to protect. As rendered in the pages of their comic, the burden of otherness became a noble sacrifice replete with sudden, unanticipated pleasures – the secret workings of the mind as overheard by the telepath Jean Grey; New York's skyline viewed from above by the winged mutant, the Angel; the imminence of rain scented five miles away on the nostrils of Storm, the African weather princess.

Should you have turned your attention away from the room's detritus on a spring day of 1982, you would have found me lying at the far end of the room flicking through Marvel Two-In-One issue 50 ('The Thing battles The Thing . . . and only one shall survive!'). Outside the tips of the fir trees thrashed in the wind. Mann Parrish's 'Hip Hop Be Bop Don't Stop' spiralled from the wooden speakers of the record player.

The room's other occupant was absent, last sighted at lunchtime loping across the school playground. At sixteen, Kodwo had legs so long they swallowed the concrete span of the playground beneath him in one, two, three giant strides. His beakish face was pushed out on its narrow neck like a baby bird keening for its mother. On his shoulders hung a second-hand tweed greatcoat that caught the wind and billowed behind him like a cape. Around his neck was a Dr Who scarf of serpentine proportions. Acquired one Saturday afternoon at Camden Market, it had barely left his presence since. Even at home he sat playing it through his hands. When he thought I wasn't looking, he'd tie its end into a knot and snap it experimentally in my direction to test how easily it bounced off my head.

The door swung open. Kodwo strode in, nodding to the music that hissed out of the orange foam headphones of his Walkman. He spilled a carrier bag of second-hand albums on to his bed. More additions to his collection of Yes, Hawkwind and Emerson, Lake and Palmer records. Without acknowledging me he skated across the carpet of comics, flicked off Mann Parrish and dropped one of the new records on to the turntable. Blasts of Moog synthesizer filled the room. He leaned over the turntable, inhaling the sound with a dreamy expression. From across the room I decided to make my presence felt.

'Kodwo, this is crap.'

'No, it's not. It's brilliant.'

'I was trying to do my homework when you came. You'll have to turn it down.'

'Liar. You're reading comics.'

'I was *about* to start doing my homework, and I can't do it with that playing.'

'If you don't like it you can get out.'

'This is my room as much as yours.'

'I'm not turning it off.'

'I'm going to tell Mum and Dad.'

'Go ahead, crybaby.'

'What you going to do? Stop me?'

'I will if I have to.'

Those were the limits of our conversations at the time. Occasionally they ended in actual blows – weak, careless things thrown by me in frustration rather than true malice. For the most part, the result was that Kodwo turned up the music while I slunk downstairs to watch *The Dukes of Hazzard*. Despite the enmity between us, there was a hierarchy to the room and to our relationship. Where he led I followed.

In the spaces of our room unoccupied by comics, piles of science-fiction paperbacks teetered towards the ceiling. Cold-eyed dystopias heaped on top of baroque fantasies, their nicotine-fumed pages testament to their origins in musty second-hand bookstores. Above them, the walls were coated in posters. Star-dappled fish swimming across an interstellar void, as painted by the progressive rock artist Roger Dean. Cornelius and Zira, the chimpanzee scientists of *Planet of the Apes*, dressed in spacesuits. A photograph of Ken Kesey and the Merry Pranksters torn from a book about the Beats showed the group flower-haired and extravagantly high, clustered round a converted school bus painted in psychedelic swirls. The destination sign on the front read 'Further'.

All of this was by Kodwo's design. He had an instinctive

notion of the uncontained universe and the room was a memorial to its possibilities – to time travel and alien races and the impossible joy of watching a superman launch himself skyward.

Instead of progressive rock I was fascinated by Afrika Bambaataa and the Soul Sonic Force, Grandmaster Flash and the Furious Five, Whodini, and the other hip-hop acts whose records would arrive by irregular dispatch from cousin Marcus in New York. Dressed in a silver cape and wraparound shades on the cover of *Planet Rock*, Bambaataa looked as if he'd been beamed to the Bronx from beyond the solar system. A former gang leader turned interstellar funklord, he proved it was possible to reimagine the boundaries of your existence. In his music the Bronx became a futurescape populated by dazzling creatures with names such as Pow Wow, Whizz Kid and G.L.O.B.E. Here were names that offered the tantalizing possibility of other galaxies beyond the mundanity of life in Kingsbury.

From what I could tell, Kodwo suffered none of my unease about our circumstances. Scientific by tempera-ment, artistic by inclination, he was disdainful of the ordinary world around him. The kids at school were morons. Pop music was crap compared to the glories of Yes. Fiction mundane unless alloyed to the fantastic. Already wreathed in self-possession, the coup led Kodwo to even loftier intemperance. He would fly into a rage midway through a discussion with me about the relative merits of Black Goliath versus Luke Cage, Power Man, or fall into a prolonged silence even while his favourite ELP album was still turning on the stereo.

I learned not to interrupt his reveries in the morning before school or late at night when he'd listen to John Peel while reading *The Drowned World* or some other science-fiction dystopia. After a while it seemed simpler not to talk to him at all. I assumed at the time that my presence in the room was enough to sour his mood. Looking back now I suspect the reason had less to do with irritation than with sorrow. Who wants to learn as a child that reality is made of something less pliant than the stuff of your dreams? This is what Kodwo discovered with the coup, when he was thirteen. The greatest indication I had of that wasn't his rotten temper, but the way I'd catch him sometimes sighing to himself with a whole shudder of his body, the sighs freighted with weariness, forbearance and the weight of too much knowledge.

By sixteen Kodwo was so self-absorbed he barely seemed to notice me. Naturally I hated him for that. With Kodwo hidden behind a book at the other end of the room, I'd find myself thinking about the disappearance of our old life. Dwelling on what we'd lost would ruin a whole evening. I could watch television, scratch at my homework, read some comics – and all the time be picturing my dad in the midnight-blue Volvo, as he slid beneath the overpass at the Museum of London. By retreating into himself Kodwo had left me alone with my own sadness. In comparison to his Reed Richards I felt as forlorn as Ben Grimm.

At eighteen Kodwo won a scholarship to Oxford to study

English. He departed one morning in a flurry of scarves and coats, a stack of science-fiction paperbacks crooked under his arm. For years I'd been waging battle against him across the sea of comics. The coup had driven him to some remote place within himself. With squabbling as my weapon, I'd hoped to bring him back to ordinary life. He wouldn't thank me, I felt, but at least things would be more like they'd been before. At least I wouldn't be alone.

With his departure I saw that even without the coup he'd have grown beyond the confines of the room. Watching him vanish out of the door I assumed that Kodwo had effected an immaculate escape from Kingsbury and the past itself. It was years before I found out how wrong I'd been.

VI

During our final year in Queensbury I had spent a half-term holiday week with my father. Each morning I rode to work with him in the midnight-blue Volvo. From the back, I could see Mr Johnson's gloved hands at the wheel steering us towards the Ghanaian High Commission in Belgravia. My father sat beside him, crackling through the newspapers and passing the *Daily Mirror* back to me so I could read *Andy Capp* and *Garth*. Behind the windows office towers and mansion blocks slipped past in a conspiracy of whispers.

Inside the High Commission, I followed my dad up the curve of the staircase to his office. The gold letters on his door read 'Attaché to the Ministry of Information'. If that title meant anything to me at eleven years old it was the understanding that authority is the opposite of exertion. My legs dangling from a leather armchair, I watched him from a corner of his office. Behind a vast desk he dictated letters to his secretaries and took calls on twin black telephones. Assistants bustled into the office with documents bearing the eagle crest of Ghana. When he signed his name at the bottom of them, the signet ring on his left hand would flare beneath the brass desk lamp.

For lunch one afternoon, he took me to the Spaghetti House in Knightsbridge. It had been the site of a siege three years before, he told me, taking off his jacket and draping it over the top of the velvet banquette. Three gunmen calling themselves the Black Liberation Front had raided the safe and locked the staff in the basement while the police massed outside. The stand-off lasted for six days until, having accepted the plane they demanded would never materialize, the robbers surrendered.

I looked round at the chequered tablecloths and the plastic grapevines twined through the rafters. My experience of restaurants was largely confined to quarter pounders at the Wimpy on Queensbury high street. For all I knew six-day stand-offs with the police were an everyday part of the adult dining experience. I nodded in what I hoped was an appropriately sage manner. Burrowing into the velvet banquette beside my father I felt swell and grown-up, as if we were two men of the world accustomed to its mysterious ways.

After spaghetti all'amatriciana there was a plate of fruit salad, which, to my delight, came fresh, not out of a tin like at home. Black grapes glimmered beneath cream like the domes of a winter palace crested with snow.

'This is great, Dad,' I said, resisting the urge to suggest we cap off the meal with a cigar each.

We went back to the High Commission. He worked while I read a library hardback of T. H. White's *The Once and Future King*, imagining myself as Wart to his Merlin.

Riding home along the Edgware Road that evening, I started to feel sick. I wanted to tell my dad to pull over, but something ominous was happening in my stomach. With abrupt force, the afternoon's spaghetti all'amatriciana and fruit salad came splashing into my lap. At the sound of retching, my father twisted round and uttered a small and distinct 'Oh' of surprise. The Volvo pulled over and he opened the back door with a box of tissues in his hand. I felt as limp as a shipwreck survivor crawling to the shore. My eyes slid shut and I passed out.

We were still riding home when I woke. My father had moved to the back and his arm was round my shoulder. I shut my eyes again. For the rest of the journey, all the world consisted of were the subterranean echoes of his belly as they rang in my ear.

My parents didn't talk about money when we moved to Kingsbury, but I knew we had none. Poverty is subjective. We were hardly destitute. Yet the comfort of 176 Beverly

Drive made our new circumstances more difficult to bear.

A while after we moved house our phone line was cut off. We couldn't afford to pay the bill, and it remained disconnected for the next eighteen months. When Jamie Brown or Benny Mitchell complained they couldn't get through I'd shrug and say there must have been a fault on the line. Even a weak lie seemed better than admitting the truth. But if I was ashamed of what we'd lost, how must my parents have felt to see everything they'd worked for vanish?

With my mother working at the hospital, my dad enrolled at City University and began a business degree. His presence filled the house. Watching him in the evening, as I lay with the fibres of the living-room carpet rubbing against my face, I wondered at how confined he felt. Now that he was limited to home, I thought he looked trapped, as if the force of him had turned in on itself.

My father and I used to go out every weekend to buy the family groceries at Sainsbury's. It was a ritual that had been in place since before the Fall. Standing in the kitchen one Saturday, I decided to break it.

'Why? You don't want to come with me?' he asked.

'I don't feel like it,' I said.

That was how it seemed to me at the time. Looking back I see that what I meant was I'd grown tired of simulating a normality that no longer existed. It was another rebellion, like dropping a plate on to the hard floor. In which case, perhaps it's not surprising my father heard a challenge to his authority.

'So you don't want to come with me?' he repeated, this time slapping me heavily across the head.

The shock of the blow more than its force set my head spinning. I staggered backwards and he cuffed me again, then repeatedly. I fell to the tiled floor. Hands around my ears I curled into a ball.

'I'll come to the shops,' I said. 'I'll come.'

He didn't seem to hear me. With my head against the tiles I saw him wrench open the cutlery drawer and heft a spatula in his hand. Dissatisfied he flung it back in the drawer, dug out a long-handled wooden spoon and started to smack me around the head and legs with its convex back.

Through streaming eyes I noticed the outline of his vest against his blue shirt, and how the black frame of his glasses sat askew on the bridge of his nose. Beneath the fluorescent light a globule of phlegm glistened on his chin. I was less aware of the pain of each blow than the sting of humiliation. At twelve years old, my ambition was to become an astronaut. But I had another, less lofty aim. I wanted to be recognized for myself instead of simply as my father's son or, at school, as a representative of All the Black People in the World. Finding myself on the kitchen floor proved I'd failed in even these modest desires. It meant I was worth nothing.

It was five years before my father got another job. After his business degree he did an MA, then started working for Brent Council. During that time I often saw him brooding and frustrated. Yet I can't look at those years with any anger because they seem to me only part of the larger measure of a man: the scud of clouds across a landscape.

As I wobbled on my first bicycle he was the person who ran alongside and held me up. In the school holidays I'd wake up early to stretch on the carpet beside him as he practised yoga. Some mornings I followed him when he went jogging. The sun still pale and the streets empty we'd work our way round Roe Green park and come home together, panting and exultant.

When I was thirteen I managed, through a mix of complacency and disaffection, to garner a report card of such horror I was convinced my life would end, swiftly and violently, when I took it home. Counting a total of thirteen Ds, five Es and a full set of must-do-betters in the comment column, I decided that drastic action was necessary. With a Bic pen I converted the grades to Bs and Cs, and presented the counterfeit to my father with a trembling hand. He looked it over, told me off for the displeased comments of my teachers, then passed it back to me. I'd got away with it. Dizzy with relief I reached out to snatch it back. Maybe it was the eagerness of that action or the glint of triumph on my face, but something made him hold on to the report. He peered closer at it and frowned. Then he held it up to the bulb, exposing the shadow of the original grades.

My mouth turned dry. I couldn't move. Downstairs, I was aware of a Road Runner cartoon playing on television. A police car raced by outside with its siren on.

My father looked down at me.

'So,' he said. 'I see.'

And that was it.

I wasn't the only one that was speechless. After his shock wore off, he had a lot more to say. It was all sympathetic, though.

In the woefulness of my grades he recognized, more clearly than I had, that I'd come to a crossroads between trying harder and abandoning effort – and maybe school itself – altogether. Possibly he saw, too, that the point I'd reached had something to do with the coup. That perhaps what I needed at that moment was someone to tell me things would be all right.

My father is in his sixties now. Age agrees with him. I spot delight on his face when we meet. We hug without self-consciousness, clinging together for a few moments longer than is necessary. His chest beats against mine. Beneath my hands I feel the broadness of his shoulders, the solidity of his frame. And I know him then to be one of the fragile creatures of this earth.

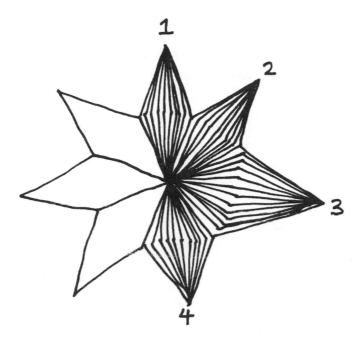

The summer of red, black and green – The discovery of the Gold Coast – The walls of Elmina castle – Inside the male slave dungeon – Through the Door of No Return – The troubled life of Jacobus Capitein

I

On my tenth day in Accra I woke up to a drowned city.

Overnight, rain clouds had barraged the streets like warplanes on a bombing mission. Daylight brought a scene of devastation. Cars lay overturned in the road. The body of a cow was discovered bloated and stinking in a back yard in Asylum Down. Alongside the Nima highway, the side of a house had caved in, offering drivers the unusual sight of a woman mopping her sodden living room in full view of the passing traffic.

I decided to get out of town.

At Kaneshi station I bought a bus ticket that would take me west along the Atlantic coastline to Elmina. The bus left that afternoon.

An air of malaise hung over the city, as if it really had been the victim of wartime catastrophe. In place of the normal commotion there was a dazed hush. Passers-by picked their way along mud-caked streets. Cars inched over rutted tarmac. As the bus grumbled out of the station I shut my eyes, and the sensation was exactly that of a boat struggling out of port against heavy waves. I clung to the armrest and let the bus carry me away from Accra and across the open sea that stretched vast and unmapped behind my eyelids.

My mind drifted.

I thought of Dwayne Hall, my tormentor at high school, and how I had never found a good answer to his question.

'Where you from?' asked Dwayne.

I still couldn't say today.

The last of Accra dropped away. The bus eased on to the highway.

When we were both fifteen Dwayne had been a head taller than me. Extra height gave him a better reach. It meant he could hold me back with one arm while pounding me in the stomach with the other. Flanked by his lieutenants Devon Mitchell and Mark Curtis, Dwayne always wore a puzzled expression as he stood over me, as if he felt obliged to carry on pummelling me even though he wasn't sure why.

'Where you from?' he'd ask, between blows.

'Oi, Kunte Kinte, where d'you live?'

'Up a tree?' added Devon Mitchell and Mark Curtis.

When I tried to answer the words would come out as hiccups of tears. Even if I'd been able to speak clearly I'm not sure what I'd have said. After they'd finished punching me, I was allowed to go back to the other side of the playground from where they'd plucked me. I could feel Dwayne watching me as I hobbled away. After a year of irregular beatings, he and his crew lost interest in me. For the most part, they stopped turning up for school altogether. So it was only with hindsight that I realized how much I envied them.

Born in England to Jamaican parents, it seemed to me they drew from their dual heritage without angst – in the patois they traded and the exercise books they stickered with the Jamaican flag. In their height, and the swagger with which they proceeded, three abreast, down the school corridor, I saw a self-assurance I could never match. For Dwayne and his crew, being West Indian and British brought with it an ineffable cool. They were the school trendsetters. The first kids with the newest style of Fila trainers or the latest Streetsounds Electro album. They were the ones who pollinated patois across the playground and created the template for a teeth-kissing disdain of adulthood adopted by the entire fourth year. Looking back I can see they belonged to a generation of young Caribbean-originated Britons making themselves heard during the early 1980s. Black sitcoms such as *No Problem* were being broadcast on television. Jazz funk singers such as Junior Giscombe and David Grant scored hits in the charts. John Barnes was scoring for England. Thanks to that generation, black people were garnering a level of popular respect in Britain they'd never before held.

Unless you came from Africa – in which case you were still nobody.

At least that's how it felt to me. After all, what kind of heritage did I have compared to Dwayne?

'Where you from?' he'd say. And all I could think of were the despots on the cover of my father's *West Africa* magazine, with their cold eyes and fly whisks. On television there were *Roots* and the African character created by Lenny Henry on *Tiswas*, with his leopard-skin fez and his catchphrase, 'Katanga!' Among the piles of comics in my bedroom, there was a solitary African superhero, the Black Panther, who stalked the rooftops of Manhattan with 'the strength and agility of a jungle cat'.

'Where you from?' Dwayne would say.

I assumed the question was rhetorical. That Africa stood for something backward in his mind. That he beat me up at lunchtime out of contempt.

Yet seeing again the look of confusion on his face, it occurs to me now that maybe he was looking for a proper answer. Perhaps the reason he picked on me was because he really *did* want to know where I was from. This is the only reason I can think of to explain why the next time I saw Dwayne he'd become a born-again African.

It was 1989. The summer London turned red, black and green. The summer of apocalyptic prophecies. An African-American professor wrote a book about the coming war between 'ice' people and 'sun' people. In the closing minutes of Spike Lee's *Do the Right Thing* the racial sparrings of a Brooklyn neighbourhood ignited into riot. The most haunting moment on Public Enemy's *It Takes a Nation of Millions to Hold Us Back* belonged to a voice calling out above a clamour of sirens: 'Freedom is a road seldom travelled by the multitude.'

It was the summer I turned twenty-one; the summer black people in Britain discovered Africa. At bookstores in Hackney you could buy stone busts of Nefertiti and leather pendants in the shape of Africa. Young men in suits and bow ties stood among the traffic on Coldharbour Lane, selling copies of the *Final Call*. Someone published a magazine called *The Sphinx* featuring a comic strip about the lives of the Pharaohs.

'Here, my brother.'

On the Edgware Road, a young black man wearing an Africa pendant thrust a photocopied leaflet into my hand.

'Read and learn,' he called after me.

Walking up the street, I turned it over. The leaflet

described a mythic time when the continent of Africa had been a single peaceful nation – Bilad as Sudan, the Land of the Blacks – where Africans had lived together in peace until the coming of the white man brought ruin and warfare. I skimmed through it hurriedly. There were many such leaflets being distributed that summer, most of them harking back to some supposedly golden period of black history. It was only after I'd shoved it into my pocket that I realized that the young man who'd handed it to me was Dwayne Hall. By then I'd lost sight of him in the crowd. I'd missed the chance to find out what had brought him to that street corner.

Had he come to ask himself the same question with which he used to interrogate me? Did the answer prove so elusive it had led him all the way back to an imaginary African past? If so, he wasn't alone. That summer, London seemed to be full of born-again Africans.

Their inspiration came from hip-hop acts such as Public Enemy and KRS One who'd resurrected the black national-ism of Malcolm X and Bobby Seale, and allied it to the infectiousness of their studio-produced beats. On the cover of *By All Means Necessary*, KRS One re-created an iconic photo of Malcolm X, the rapper staring through the cur-tains of a window as if under siege, an Uzi submachine gun clutched at his side.

Listening to the swarm of sirens, horns and slogans on a Public Enemy track felt like tuning into the broadcasts of a state at war with itself. Reproduced on pendants, T-shirts and photocopied handouts, Africa had become the symbol of a renewed wave of black political consciousness.

I read through Dwayne's leaflet again. As black people we came from royal blood, it said. 'Raise your heads, brothers and sisters. You are kings and queens joined by spiritual values. Children of the sun and descendants of the Pharaohs.' I threw it away with a sigh. Dwayne and his crew used to tell me I lived in a tree. Now he wanted to remind me about my regal past. The trouble was I felt no more noble than I ever had bestial.

All the same, spurred by hip-hop, black people really did raise their heads that summer. The mood of empowerment within rap found an echo in music and film on both sides of the Atlantic. The multicultural collective Soul II Soul emerged from its studios in Camden Town with a million-selling album and a utopian belief in the unifying powers of music, clubs and high fashion. At art-house cinemas you could catch screenings of black British independent films such as *Handsworth Songs* and *The Passion of Remembrance*. In New York, De La Soul, the Jungle Brothers and A Tribe Called Quest crafted a rhapsodic take on hip-hop built on the premise of racial tolerance and creative promiscuity. I went to the Notting Hill Carnival that year wearing a T-shirt emblazoned with a red, black and green image of Africa. Dancing with the crowd at Norman Jay's Good Times sound system a feeling seized me that all of us there, in that assemblage of skin colours and histories, represented something good and hopeful about London and Britain itself.

Carnival takes place on the last weekend of August, and

it traditionally represents the end of summer. For a long while afterwards the optimism of those months stayed with me. Every time I collected another leaflet like Dwayne's, I pictured myself dancing beside Norman Jay's speaker stacks and how the crowd there had seemed to articulate a belief in a multicultural future instead of the prejudices of the Britain I'd known growing up.

Forget about the future – the trouble with those leaflets was they couldn't even deal with the contradictions of the present. Reading yet another call for black people to 'know their past' made me think of Ghana, where seventy-five different languages were spoken by a collection of ethnic groups who'd spent most of their history at war with each other. Then I tried to multiply those divisions across the fifty-four countries and 800 million inhabitants of this huge continent.

When I was done I couldn't look at an Africa pendant without getting angry. What was the point of a black consciousness based on mystification? We were not royal by birth. We were not bound by spiritual values. We had come from a place as fierce and strange and ordinary as any other part of the world. That was the truth. Why couldn't it be enough?

'Where you from?'

The question had never gone away. Was I any closer to resolving it now that I'd finally returned to Africa?

II

The bus arrived in Elmina at sundown. Shouldering my
rucksack, I walked through lanterned streets, past shop-
keepers in their doorways and fishermen hawking the
remains of their catch – spiny tilapia, rose-hued mullet, the
formless grey flesh of some giant mollusc splayed on
oilcloth like an afterbirth. By the time I found a hotel, night
had fallen. My room overlooked a harbour. Through the
darkness I could hear the sound of water slapping against
the hull of fishing canoes.

Although I was worn out from the journey I couldn't
sleep. I dug out my guide book. It told me that during
the eighteenth century, the Ghanaian shore was the site
of the densest accumulation of European forts in African
history. The largest of these was São Jorge castle, built by
the Portuguese here at Elmina in 1482; however, there
had been more than fifty others stretched along the 300-
mile coastline. Most of them belonged to Holland and
England, with the remainder built by Portugal, Denmark
and Sweden, as well as three others erected in a spirit of
adventurism by the state of Brandenburg. What drew all
these nations to Africa was trade. In the late sixteenth
century, the value of gold shipped annually from West
Africa was £100,000, or 10 per cent of the world supply.

There is so much gold in Elmina, wrote the Dutch
merchant Pieter De Marees in 1602, that villagers dive to
the bottom of the river and scoop it up with their bare

hands. For European merchants the opening up of Africa sparked a frenzy similar in kind to later dashes for profit such as the South Sea Bubble and the dotcom boom.

From Holland alone twenty vessels a year were weighing anchor at Elmina by the 1590s. Between them, they carried 200,000 yards of linen, 100,000 pounds of beads and 40,000 pounds of copper basins, as well as earthenware pots, brass cauldrons, barbers' basins, looking glasses, stuffed horsetails for use as fly swatters, iron bars to forge into machetes, and the vibrantly coloured Venetian glass beads prized on the coast as jewellery.

Trade with Africans did not always prove straightforward, though. The earliest Europeans on the coast came from Portugal. For decades they gulled the local people with rusty basins, mouldy cloth and other poor-quality goods, before being finally driven out by their enraged hosts. Faced with renewed waves of white men, the Africans came to pride themselves on their perspicacity as customers. Bolts of linens were rolled out on the ground to check for mildew; cauldrons kicked to test against buckling; knives examined for rust. Unembarrassed about introducing their own sharp practices, the Africans sprinkled copper into gold dust, coated lumps of tin with gold veneer and melted the Europeans own coins into bracelets which they sold back to them as solid gold.

What can Africa have made of the Europeans who arrived on its shores? For all that they communicated through trade, the white men would have remained as freakish a spectacle as Martians landing in Leicester

Square. In 1742 – some 200 years after a trade route was established – the sight of Europeans was still enough to cause consternation among local people.

The Ghanaian historian C. C. Reindorff records the meeting that year between King Frempung of the Akim people and a Danish merchant, Nicolas Kamp. Received by courtiers at the Akim palace, Kamp made a low bow before the king, who sat surrounded by his wives. With a cry, Frempung hurled himself to the ground. Guards held back the visitor. The king's wives formed a circle around his prone form. Until then, he had never seen a white man. As Kamp bowed, Frempung had caught sight of the merchant's pigtail. It had looked to him like an actual tail sprouting from his neck. Raised on stories that white men lived at sea and survived on raw flesh he had taken fright.

Tentatively, Frempung's head emerged from behind the women. Across the palace floor, the Dane explained that he was no animal. Frempung demanded he strip naked to prove it. Kamp took off his shirt. Tentatively, Frempung approached. He ran a hand across the merchant's chest and prodded a finger in his belly. Then he stood back and looked him up and down.

'You really are a human,' said the king. 'But as white as the devil.'

III

In the year 1749 a male slave bought at Elmina castle was worth six ounces of gold payable in equivalent goods. These were listed in the ledgers of the Dutch West India Company as the following:

2 muskets
40 pounds gunpowder
1 anker brandy
1 piece cotton cloth
1 piece patterned Indian cloth
1 piece plain Indian cloth
2 pieces gingham
2 iron rods
1 copper rod
4 pieces fine linen
1,000 beads
1 pewter basin
20 pounds cowrie shells

The castle was built by 600 Portuguese soldiers, sailors, carpenters and masons who landed at Elmina on the morning of Wednesday, 19 January 1482. It was a clear, warm day and contemporary accounts record that, after negotiations between Diego d'Azambuja, the Portuguese commander, and Kwamina Ansa, the king of Elmina, construction work began the following day. Like the other coastal forts that followed Elmina, its initial function was trade – copper pots, beads and brandy for ivory, pepper and gold. But by 1700 the nature of that commerce had shifted.

A report from the Dutch West India Company in 1730 noted that 'the part of Africa which as of old is known as the "Gold Coast" . . . has now virtually changed into a pure Slave Coast.'

At Elmina, control of the castle had fallen to the Dutch. Holland required manpower to work the new plantations it was establishing in the Caribbean. The same demands for labour were repeated at the British forts along the coast. In answer, almost a million slaves were exported from Ghana to the New World – over a fifth of the 4.5 million people shipped in total from West Africa during the eighteenth century, when the slave trade was at its peak.

As the oldest and largest of the European forts, Elmina marked the epicentre of the slave trade in Ghana. The castle was the reason I'd travelled to Elmina. I wanted to see the site of slavery for myself.

Early the next morning I wandered through Elmina's narrow streets. The town smelled of wood smoke and old age. Nineteenth-century colonial buildings stood next to wooden huts with corrugated steel roofs. A herd of goats ambled down an empty lane. I turned a corner near the harbour and found the castle. Its walls were freshly whitewashed and they rose, futuristic-looking amid the huts, like the remnants of an alien intelligence.

I crossed the drawbridge and entered a courtyard the scale of which seemed to exist only to remind you of your insignificance. Battlements stretched into the sky. Beyond them I could hear waves dash against the shore. The sound was remote, as if the castle's presence had cowed the sea. Across the flagstones, I saw an arched doorway marked with a painted skull and crossbones. A sign above read 'Male Slave Dungeon'.

I ducked beneath the arch and descended along a sloping passage. The light receded behind me. The air became heavy and damp. I ran my hand along the wall. It came away coated in green algae. At the end of the passage I emerged into the dungeon. The light from a small window high up on the wall percolated the gloom. The cell was the size of a school classroom. It used to hold 300 slaves at a time, the dying locked in with the living. All the prisoners breathing the same feculent air. All of them defecating on the flagstones that, over time, became coated with a solid layer of sand and human waste.

Alone in the cell I felt the air press upon me like a physical weight. I pictured what it was like for a slave to be herded into the courtyard after spending months in the dungeon.

A Dutch ship is weighing anchor. You are brought into the light and made to strip naked. For the first time in a long while you are aware of your body's scent in all its sourness. A soldier shaves your head with a straight razor. He has a young face and ruined teeth. He nicks your scalp with the razor. The Dutch captain enters the courtyard.

He is balding and impatient. He sticks his fingers in your mouth to check for loose teeth. You taste his sweat on your tongue. The captain rejects the sick among you as damaged goods. The rest of you are lined up before a brazier. You are branded on the shoulder. The smell of burnt skin is almost as hard to bear as the pain itself.

They clamp a ring round your neck, thread a chain through it and tug you all in line to a narrow exit at the far end of the courtyard. It is called the 'Door of No Return'. One by one you step through. The ocean lies in front of you. Struggling against the chains you and the other men are walked to the waiting boat, then rowed out to the ship. You are unshackled in order to climb aboard. Some men throw themselves in the water and try to swim for land. The ones who don't drown are captured on their return. The rest of you are counted and taken down into the hold. The ship raises anchor. It turns away from Africa and ploughs across the sea. Turns away from the known world, as it seems in the blindness of the hold.

I left the dungeon, the light stinging my eyes as I returned to the courtyard. Beyond the castle walls fishermen banged buckets to announce the arrival of the day's catch. A goat maintained a solitary bleating. I smelled the salt of the ocean. For a few minutes it was all I could do to stand bent over, gulping air, until the weight of the dungeon had left my shoulders. When I raised my eyes I saw it across the courtyard: the Door of No Return. It was cut into the wall at the far side of the castle. Except for the sign it could have passed for an ordinary archway.

I stood beside it and ran my hands along the stonework. I stepped through it as the slaves had done, to the shoreline and the waves. As I did, it came to me that, in the wake of slavery, all of us black people born in the west are exiles. Periodically, Elmina stages a 'homecoming' ceremony where African-Americans, Caribbeans and black Europeans are invited back through the Door of No Return to the land of their origins.

Is it possible to reclaim the past? Or do we remain wanderers even after our return? This is what Jacobus Capitein, vicar of Elmina castle, must have asked himself time and again when he gazed out from the castle walls. I'd read about Capitein the previous evening, and the course of his troubled life came back to me as I stood with my back to the door.

Capitein was a Ghanaian boy of eight years old when he was kidnapped by slavers trawling the coast in 1725. They sold him to the captain of a Dutch frigate who, in turn, gave him as a present to Jacobus Van Goch, the West India Company representative at the Dutch fort of St Sebastian. It was Van Goch who named the boy Capitein (Captain), after the frigate commander, and who discovered him to be hard-working, eager to please and good-natured. After three years in the Gold Coast, Van Goch returned to The Hague, Capitein beside him as an adopted son.

In the notes that survive him to this day, Capitein claimed he was unable to remember his real name or the village where he was born. Whether this is true or an act of willed forgetting is impossible to say. What it makes clear is that he regarded the moment of his enslavement as the start of a new life. In that respect he may have considered himself European even before he and Van Goch landed in The Hague. If so, the reaction to him in Holland must have been a disappointment. In his notes, Capitein writes that mothers hurried their children across the street as he approached. Strangers pointed. Young men deliberately jostled him as they passed.

In the quiet of the Haagsche Bosch park, he'd find a bench where he could sit alone and escape the taunts of 'blackamoor' that followed him through the city. Slavery was illegal within the borders of eighteenth-century Holland and, as a free citizen, Capitein became the first African baptized in the Netherlands. At the Dutch Reform church in Kloosterkerk he took the name Jacobus Elisa Johannes Capitein, after his adoptive father's family.

On completing school, Capitein left The Hague to study theology at the University of Leiden. He made friends among the students and gained a reputation for diligence and generosity. A portrait from that time shows him dressed in a university gown, clutching a Bible. The softness of his expression and fullness of his belly give the impression of a man at ease with himself.

Yet the painting captures Capitein at a pivotal period of life. Shortly after he began university, Van Goch had died. With a small stipend from his will, Capitein was free to determine his own future. Even if he regarded himself as completely European he need no longer have rejected his

African past. Instead Capitein continued to insist he had no memory of his early childhood. Moreover, for his graduation thesis he decided to write a paper in defence of slavery.

When *A Political-Theological Dissertation On Slavery As Not Being Contrary to Christian Freedom* was published in March 1742, it created a sensation. Africa was a land of heathens, wrote Capitein. In transporting its people to the New World, Europeans were bringing souls from darkness into the light of civilization. They were performing God's will. Morally speaking, slavery was an act of liberation.

In a country that had grown rich off slavery while agonizing over the trade's ethics, Capitein's argument found fervent support. A first print run of the dissertation sold out in weeks. Three more followed the same year. Framed portraits of him went on sale in bookshop windows and found their way on to display above mantelpieces across Holland. Capitein undertook a nationwide tour of Dutch Reform churches. Parishioners clamoured for a glimpse of the 'Africaansche Moor'.

At the peak of his celebrity, however, he decided to return to the Gold Coast. He was going back out of a sense of duty, said Capitein. Van Goch had lifted him out of ignorance and it was his responsibility to do the same for other less fortunate souls on the Dark Continent.

In light of his dissertation's success, the West India Company and the Council of the Dutch Reform Church in Amsterdam appointed him vicar of Elmina castle. In

July 1742 he sailed from the north-western island of Texel, on the slave ship *Catherine Galey*, accompanied only by the indifferent verse of his university friends: 'Your departure is bitter for me, O black Moor, internally much whiter than alabaster.'

As Holland slid out of sight, did Capitein imagine himself leaving home or returning to it? What did Africa hold for him? And what, once he reached his destination, would he discover about himself?

IV

Thinking about Capitein led me to remember the day my family moved out of Kingsbury. I'd already left home for university by then. With Esi and Kodwo gone before me, my parents decided to clear the debts they'd built up after the coup by moving to Northampton.

I went back that Christmas in 1987 to box up the records and comics still piled in the bedroom Kodwo and I had shared. When we'd finished and the removal van had rumbled off towards the M1, we squeezed into the back of the second-hand Beetle my father had bought as a replacement for the Volvo.

'Better take a last look,' he said. 'Because we won't be coming back.' Then he pulled into the traffic and away from the house for good.

At the time I thought him cruel, but his brusqueness makes sense now as a desire to leave the memory of the coup years behind. He was right, too. We didn't return. Not, at least, until years later when I took myself on a sentimental journey back to Kingsbury. Somehow I expected to spot old school friends hanging outside the kebab shop or sneaking fags under the bus shelter as they'd been doing the last time I saw them. But there was no one I recognized and, gazing up at the net-curtained windows of the old house, I felt nothing beyond the shallow wash of nostalgia.

It seems to me now that the act of departure affects the nature of the place you leave behind. Between leaving and coming back, you change. And because you don't stay the same, neither does the place to which you return.

When Capitein was baptized in Holland, he renounced Africa. What drew him back? Did he accept he'd always be a stranger in Holland, or was he searching for his lost childhood? Perhaps both were true, even if Capitein himself viewed matters differently.

His actions in the first weeks suggest a man little given to introspection. In the space of a fortnight he set up a school for African children at the castle, recruited his first twenty pupils and began translating the Lord's Prayer into Fante. His mission, as he saw it, was not to get closer to the Africans, but to bring them nearer to Europe. To further prove that he 'did not despise them', Capitein also decided to marry a young woman from Elmina.

As he would have discovered on his arrival, West India Company rules forbidding relationships with African women were commonly flouted at the castle. Most of the

Dutch officers kept an African mistress at the fort. Their light-skinned children were a common sight in the streets of Elmina. All the same, his request was turned down by Jacob de Petersen, Director-General of the castle. In protest Capitein appealed to the company in Holland, arguing that a wife would help secure him against 'the seductions of Satan'.

It took two years for him to receive a reply. In 1745 a young red-haired woman named Antonia Ginderos arrived on a ship from The Hague. She announced herself as Capitein's fiancée. Without his knowledge, the West India Company had arranged a bride for the vicar.

Although they'd never previously met the couple were married at the castle by de Petersen shortly after her arrival. In a letter of gratitude to the Council of the Dutch Reform Church, Capitein described her as his 'gift from God'. After two years in Elmina, though, there was little else for him to celebrate.

Prim and sanctimonious, Capitein was unpopular with the rest of the castle staff. His fellow officers were coarse, illiterate, heavy drinkers, less used to regarding Africans as equals than as slaves and whores. At an official dinner, de Petersen's aide-de-camp called the vicar a 'filthy nigger'. Capitein tried to ignore him, but the invective continued. None of the officers intervened. From their smiles, they appeared to be enjoying the scene. Capitein left the table. Afterwards he was ostracized by the staff, who claimed he couldn't take a joke. On Sundays he preached to empty pews. Attendance at his school foundered. The children would be better off working, their parents insisted. Able to speak only halting Fante, Capitein could not convince them otherwise.

With disinterest from the town and hostility at the castle, Capitein wrote despairingly to the West India Company: 'I believe that things are going to go with me the same way they must have gone with most of, if not all, my predecessors: namely that they had to toil and expend their energies fruitlessly, and to suffer the hatred, contempt, ridicule and persecution of the depraved Christians here.'

In July 1745 he followed the letter with another one offering his resignation. With no response from the company, Capitein succumbed to despair. He began to spend freely on imported wines and cloths, hoping to trade them locally for a profit. As a way to supplement their incomes many of the officers did the same, borrowing money from middlemen to purchase their initial stock. Capitein followed them, only to find himself sinking into debt. To escape his losses, he turned to the one truly profitable source of commerce on the Gold Coast. He began to buy and sell slaves.

Yet still his losses seemed to grow. On 27 December 1746 he was summoned to court in Elmina with debts of 8,447 guilders. Three days later he faced a further claim of 1,200 guilders from a local innkeeper and 79 guilders from a wine trader in Amsterdam. His reply forms his last recorded words.

'I do not have it!' he told the court. 'Sell my bed; it's no shame to me. Let those who wish to claim money be anxious, and not those in debt.'

Two months later, on 1 February 1747, Capitein was found dead, aged thirty.

In the West India Company minutes of October 1747, his demise was noted under 'Other Business'. No cause of death was given. At the castle there was no tombstone laid to mark his grave. Such indifference suggests that Capitein probably committed suicide, an act regarded at the time as a mortal sin.

Having argued the case for slavery in Leiden, Capitein returned to Africa where he saw the reality of the trade for the first time. Each year 5,000 slaves were bought and sold at the castle. From his rooms, he'd have watched as they were made to strip naked in the courtyard and marched through the Door of No Return. At what point did he start to question his former certainties?

Capitein claimed to have forgotten the African family to which he was born. Each day he faced a reminder of his past. As he gazed down into the courtyard, perhaps the former slave asked himself if he'd ever truly been free.

Leaning beside the Door of No Return, the memory of Capitein prompted me to ask why *I'd* returned to Ghana. If I was looking for somewhere I belonged, why come to a country where I'd lived for only a few years as a kid? Perhaps because the truth of a place doesn't lie in the minutiae of childhood so much as in understanding the hold that the past maintains over the present.

Going home is easy. The hard part is what happens after you arrive.

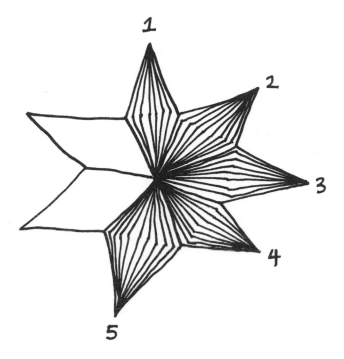

The wild spree of Horace de Graft Johnson – Escaping the past   Death and marriage on the Gold Coast   Great uncle Nana Banyin – The two sons of Joseph de Graft – The Negro Prince of Prussia – The morality of slavery

I

After two days in Elmina, I rode by bus along the shore to Cape Coast to visit West de Graft Hall, the house where my mother grew up along with eight brothers and sisters, and some thirty cousins, aunts, grandparents and other more remote relatives. A nineteenth-century flat-fronted town house that stands four storeys tall, it has sixteen rooms. Most of these housed an entire family, with the result that the place always thronged with adults chatting in the corridors, children playing riotous games in the back yard and groups of visitors in Kente cloth who'd hired the second-floor reception rooms for weddings and parties.

It was constructed in the 1890s by my mother's grand-father J. W. de Graft Johnson, who used the fortune he had made trading silk to build a house for each of his four wives. Wealth elevated J. W. into the company of Cape Coast aristocrats such as press magnate James Hutton Brew and the lawyer Joseph Ephraim Casely Hayford, who thought of themselves as the country's natural rulers after the British – 'the intelligent sons of the native soil'. His ascension to their ranks proved short-lived, however. While overseeing logging work on his lands in Assin Beraku in 1898, J. W. was knocked unconscious by a falling ebony tree. He died on his servants' shoulders as they carried him back to Cape Coast on a makeshift stretcher.

The obituary in the *Gold Coast Leader* described J. W. as a 'man of fire and action who was all bustle, hustle and rustle'. After his death, though, his son Horace, a creature of fabulous indolence, became head of the household. On coming into his inheritance Horace took up a suite of rooms on the second floor of West de Graft Hall and devoted himself to the satiation of his many appetites.

Each morning at seven it was my mother's job to run to the United Africa Company store on the high street and buy a brace of Scottish kippers, which Horace would attack over a copy of the *Cape Coast Monitor*. After breakfast, draped in the woven cloth and gold sandals of a chief, he would be 'available' to visitors. Shuffling up the stairs to his rooms would come a line of local petitioners, seeking help with their dilemmas of money and honour.

By night Horace shucked off respectability and surrendered to his baser pleasures. Drinking, gambling, roaring a wild spree through town, he acquired four wives and a couple of mistresses, lost lavishly at cards, gifted away houses on the promise of a kiss and, by the time of his death, managed to squander the whole of J. W. de Graft Johnson's considerable fortune.

All of this was to the great annoyance of Robert Newton, my mother's father, who was raising nine children on his government salary as an agricultural officer. Robert Newton: his paintbrush moustache and balding head; his high-waisted trousers and the sweet, musty scent of his pipe tobacco. He and my mother shared a love of books. In the evenings a young Adelaide would clamber into his lap and describe the unfolding events of her storybook in great and precise detail. In return he pulled a hardback from his shelves and revealed its dramas to her, so that by the time she started secondary school she knew as much about Prospero and Helen of Troy as she did the folk tales of Anansi. When her father was at work, she stretched out on one of the thick stone windowsills and found horses and angels in the clouds, and imagined the house itself as a mutable place, a palace or an ocean liner bearing her to the azure horizon.

I'd visited the house once before, as a child. Most of the families had moved on by then. The upper floors were empty and sliding towards dilapidation. I arrived with my mother by bus from Accra. We walked to the house through Kotokuraba market.

'Stay close to me,' she said, disappearing instantly into the crowd. I trailed after her, squeezing past the thighs of the market women and ducking the outstretched arms of the hawkers eager for a victim on whom to demonstrate the virtues of their patent cure-alls. The white haze of cooking fires drifted overhead, carrying with it the scent of seared goat meat.

I caught up with my mother and followed her up the rise of Coronation Street to where the house stood at the crest of the slope. We'd come to visit her parents, but as Robert Newton opened the door I was already trying to wriggle past him and go exploring. My mother shot me a warning look. I stayed put. Squirming beside her on the sofa I endured a minor lifetime of grown-up small talk before she allowed me to slip away. Leaving the adults behind I ran upstairs, their voices receding behind me as I climbed.

With no money for maintenance after Horace's free-spending years, the upper floors had been shut down. Amid the deserted rooms, I discovered a wall hung with portraits of J. W. de Graft Johnson and other family members in stiff white collars. Some of the pictures were printed on china plates. The images had faded over time, so that, on one plate, only a pair of eyes was visible. The flared nostrils of another face peeked out of a gloaming as if their owner was drawing a last breath of life as the shadow realm beckoned.

Clambering into the attic with the help of a rickety ladder, I discovered a huge space apparently unoccupied since J. W.'s time. In the jumble of broken chairs and worn-out rugs, the whole place swirling with dust, I found yellowed editions of the *Gold Coast Nation* and letters written in dense cursive script written on notepaper bearing J. W.'s personal crest, a tiger crouching. A catalogue advertising the sale of antique English shooting pistols lay on the floor, along with a children's atlas illustrated with drawings of angry-looking Russians in fur hats and smiling Negroes wearing loincloths.

I heard my mother calling from the floor below. I climbed down the stairs covered with dust and received a scolding. But as I see that scene again in my mind, I imagine myself staying up there for good. Beyond the attic dust falls like snow. Over millennia time sighs to a halt. Up in the attic I stay preserved at five years old for ever, just as the remnants of past lives have lain undisturbed for generations.

II

When I was twenty I used to say I couldn't remember my childhood. It was a surprisingly convincing lie. I even believed it myself.

With hindsight it's clear to me that it wasn't the facts of the past I was keen to avoid so much as their sensibility. I thought of the black-and-white minstrels and the kids at school tugging my hair. I heard my parents whispering about the coup and pictured Kodwo and me arguing in our comic-strewn bedroom. These things I recalled with a combination of shame and anger and regret. And at some point, I decided I'd rather forget about them altogether.

This is easily done when you are a student. On the day I started university at the London School of Economics, I waved goodbye to my parents, then, dragging a suitcase on its recalcitrant wheels to Kingsbury tube station, caught the underground to Russell Square. By the time I'd arrived at the Georgian terrace square in Bloomsbury where my hall of residence stood I was a different person.

Many students try to cut a dash through their first year with the help of an experimental haircut, a new-found political conviction or some other affectation. A wealthy Malaysian girl would arrive at LSE every day in full riding gear. Another kid, born in London to Middle Eastern parents, found himself on the front page of the *Sun* ('Ban This Mad Mullah') after a series of fiery speeches at the student union. Everyone was changing their accent or ditching the hometown sweetheart to whom they'd sworn everlasting fidelity. Everyone was looking for a new identity.

As for me, I favoured omission rather than reinvention. By shrugging off queries about where I'd grown up or gone to school, I realized that I could erase the past. Even the question that had dogged me all through life became unimportant.

'Where you from, man?'

'London.'

'Cool.'

'You heard the new Public Enemy album?'

The deadpanning of identity: it started as a conscious strategy and evolved into a habit. After a while I didn't notice what I was doing any more.

When I had left school I'd severed contact with every one of my old friends. With my parents move to Northampton during Christmas of the first term, there was nothing left to physically connect me to my childhood. Where was I from? London: that's all you needed to know. Not Kingsbury or Accra; neither English nor Fante. Now that we've cleared that up, let's talk about something that really matters. 'How's that Public Enemy album?'

Congratulations were in order. By simply refusing to believe in its force, I believed I'd evaded history. The future stretched untroubled before me. That was the plan anyway, and for a while it seemed to be working.

Through a well-connected friend at LSE, I began hanging out at a grubby office in Camden. From there, some of the capital's best club DJs, such as Norman Jay, Gilles Peterson, Jazzie B and Trevor Nelson, broadcast dance music every weekend as the pirate radio station Kiss FM. Having grown up with Kodwo's prog rock collection, the amount I knew about rare groove or New Jersey garage was minimal. Like LSE, though, Kiss struck me as a place of reinvention. Many of the DJs arrived at the station as small men, griping about money and girlfriends, and the other low blows life had struck them. Seat them behind a microphone, though, and their voices would deepen and their backs become straight. Beneficent to the listeners, wise in their selection of records, for the two hours of a show they were magisterial. Afterwards they packed up their records and slunk back into the straitened course of their existence.

I kept my mouth shut around them until I'd learned enough to talk with less than total ignorance about music. After a few months of loitering, they made me a reporter on a fifteen-minute weekend news show. I had a microphone and a tape recorder, and between lectures I'd go out and pester a visiting US rapper such as KRS One into giving me an interview. In my second year, Kiss closed down as a pirate to apply for a legal broadcasting licence. With the knowledge I'd gleaned from there I rang *The Face* magazine and began contributing small 200-word pieces about music and clubs.

Not without pride I regarded myself as a self-made man; an outsider turned initiate into the glamorous London of warehouse parties, white label 12s and evanescent fashion trends. I'd snubbed history and triumphed. That was the plan, anyway. Later, I realized that by denying the past I risked making myself its prisoner. By then it was too late, though. I was already trapped.

In the same way that I'd left Hannah, I'd spent most of my life afraid to get too close to anyone. At LSE I told myself I was being cool. With Hannah I explained it as a matter of survival. Whatever the rationale, the end result was the same. I remained alone. Just as I'd fantasized in J. W. de Graft Johnson's attic, time had moved on while I'd stayed the same. Yet however much I denied them the memories of my childhood had not faded. They'd burrowed into my psyche. They'd come to control me – in my fear of intimacy; in the jealousy I felt towards Kodwo; in my sadness at the coup. Far from escaping the past, I walked with it every day.

The upper windows of West de Graft Hall had been boarded up in the years since my last visit. As I walked up Coronation Street towards the house I saw that the front door was chipped and weathered. I ducked round the side into the back yard. Three elderly women were crouched round a cooking fire preparing a saucepan of palm nut soup. There were still a few remaining tenant families occupying the ground floor of the house, but none of them was a direct relative. I waved at the women and carried on walking. They murmured after me in Fante, then turned their attention back to the saucepan. I opened the back door and let myself in. Ahead of me lay a passageway lined with closed doors. I climbed a set of sagging stairs to the first floor, then the hall on the second floor that families used to hire for wedding receptions. The china-plate portraits that had hung there were gone. It was empty and dusty, the floorboards rotting and the walls peeled back to raw plaster.

I remembered a photograph my mother once showed me. It was shot in the yard behind the house. She and her brothers and sisters were gathered together before the camera; the youngsters in front included the twins, Peyin and Kakra, holding hands, eyes startled at the mystery of their aliveness. In the row behind stood my mother, a gamine twelve years old, regarding the camera with furious concentration. Robert Newton sat at their centre, a look of exhaustion and pride on his face.

I'd hoped to find an echo of those lives by returning to West de Graft Hall. I thought I might hear the ghosts of children running through the corridors or wedding parties dancing in the hall, but I saw now that it was just a deserted building. I traced a lattice of cracks along the wall with my finger until I found the place they coalesced to one point.

I'd spent my adult life running from my childhood. I shunned intimacy. I lived by myself and worked alone. Yet suppose it didn't have to be that way? What if the past wasn't a singular burden? What if home wasn't a place at all, but a nexus of histories? Perhaps it was more like the cracks on this wall as they came together to a single point? Something to be shared not suffered alone.

Stupid, really. Until then, I hadn't understood what

brought me to Ghana. Home was only part of it. There was something else as well, now that I thought about it. I was also searching for me.

III

I left West de Graft Hall and walked up through Cape Coast until I came to a nineteenth-century town house made of pale pink stone that stood on a hill overlooking the streets below. It was built by John Coleman de Graft Johnson, J. W.'s brother, and like West de Graft Hall it looked beaten down by time and weather.

A door stood open round the side of the house, forming a dark rectangle against the sun's glare. I knocked, stepped inside and found myself in a long, narrow hall, the floor patterned in a chequerboard of black-and-white tiles. Two easy chairs with faded green silk cushions stood together against the wall. The hall felt cool and noiseless, as I imagined a bank vault would, once you unwound its circular locks and swung open its steel door.

From a side door at the other end of the hall the owner of the house emerged. He had white hair and a face on which was written the same grace and exhaustion as his house. He crossed the chequerboard hallway and clasped my hands in his.

'I've been expecting you,' he said, standing back to look me over.

When I knew I was visiting Cape Coast, I'd arranged to

see him through my mother. His name was Nana Banyin de Graft Johnson, son of the late Horace de Graft Johnson. He was my great-uncle.

'Nana Banyin' was an honorific title. In Fante it means 'grandfather', and this struck me as appropriate because, for many years, he had been compiling an account of the sprawling de Graft Johnson genealogy that drew together all the multiple wives and obscure relatives, all the children that careered through West de Graft Hall, all the dead sons and forgotten aunts.

Nana Banyin retreated to the back of the hall and returned with a carafe of water and two glasses. He placed it between the chairs and waved at me to sit down. Side by side in the hall, we talked for the whole afternoon. Through him I discovered who the founder of my mother's family line was. And from the legal documents Nana Banyin showed me I also found out what he did for a living.

Afterwards, when I'd said goodbye and returned to the afternoon sunlight, my head was ringing. I leaned against a wall overwhelmed by anger and astonishment. I wasn't sure where I was any more. The streets looked the same. But I knew now that another reality lay beneath them.

This fact struck me as both awful and funny. Beside the bust of Queen Victoria on London Bridge, I started laughing long and hard. But there was no mirth to the sound. People hurried past afraid to meet my eye for fear I was drunk or delusional. I wanted to call out and say, 'Everything you know is wrong.' Just as quickly, though, it struck me that perhaps it was just me who was ignorant.

The past had caught up with me in Nana Banyin's mansion. It revealed itself as a joke hundreds of years in the telling. And here's what was funny: the punch line was on me.

IV

When the Europeans first built their forts on the shoreline of Ghana they discovered the climate bore a variety of infections ranging from the fatal – malaria, dysentery, yellow fever – to the bizarre – such as the Guinea worm, the larvae of which were ingested through stagnant water, and grew to three feet inside the body before chewing their way through the skin to daylight. Even worse was the mysterious '48 Hour Disease'. It began with headaches and vomiting. The next day, convulsions. By thirty-six hours pustules sprouted on the sufferer's forehead and calves, after which a lethal fever set in. No one knew what caused it or how to cure it. The only certainty was that a healthy white man would be dead precisely two days after contracting it.

Such infections probably account for the low quality of recruits serving as soldiers at the forts. Drunkards, gamblers and former convicts enlisted from across Europe, they signed on for a three-year term, with more than half dying in the first twelve months. The rest found themselves serving out their time in overcrowded barracks that leaked in the rainy season and proved hot and airless during the dry months. Fed on salt pork and hard biscuits, trapped behind a raised drawbridge at night, they fought and gambled and drank rum to battle the tedium.

The officers and company merchants of the forts had comparatively better food and conditions. As Capitein discovered at Elmina, many of them also took African concubines. Usually officially prohibited, it was nonetheless tacitly accepted by fort commanders. The most progressive marriage terms existed at the Danish fort of Christianborg in Accra, where Bishop Worm of Copenhagen had given officers a special tropical dispensation to wed African women. Danes were even required to sign over a percentage of their wages to their wives if they had children together.

Of necessity many such marriages were short-lived. Husbands either returned to Europe after their term or died on the coast. Marriages were, in any case, designed for the convenience of Europeans. An African wife could be dismissed at any time of a white man's choosing. Even so, local families were keen for their daughters to secure a white husband. Marriage was a business relationship. Through a white man, the family gained access to the forts, where they could barter goods such as gold and ivory for beads and rum. Children of mixed marriages took their father's name, and when husbands returned to Europe they would sometimes leave behind a sum of money for their African family.

This was how it went when my great-great-great-great-great-grandfather arrived from Holland. His name was

Joseph de Graft. He was a white man who arrived in Cape Coast around the 1750s and soon after married a woman named Jyemsiwa. She was a chief's daughter from the neighbouring town of Wineba. Dutch ideas of the time compared Africans to animals, which makes me wonder if he would have felt anything like love for her. But maybe Joseph came to look at things differently once he settled on the Gold Coast? Perhaps the ordinary dignity of the Africans contrasted well with the boorishness of the white men he met there? Or maybe he was just grateful for human contact when faced with the omnipresence of disease? Joseph and Jyemsiwa had a son, whom they named Joseph. He was born in 1756. A few years later, a second boy, William, followed.

I doubt that Joseph showed the same affection for Africans in general that he did his wife and children. The slave trade has never been known as a refuge for the sentimental, after all. And it was trade that had drawn Joseph across the ocean to Africa. Every three months a ship arrived from Holland, bearing his silks and copperware and schnapps in the hold. In exchange for them, Joseph bartered the slaves he'd stored in the dungeons of Elmina castle, who were taken to the Dutch plantations of the East Indies and worked until their death.

With his children still young Joseph returned to Holland. We might speculate on the reasons why. A drying up of profits, maybe? Or a letter from home? Could there have been another Mrs de Graft waiting for his return? Whatever the reason, once he left the Gold Coast Joseph never returned. To his children he bequeathed his name, de Graft. It was an entitlement that enabled Joseph, his elder son, to take up his father's occupation.

What's it like to discover your ancestor was a slave trader?

As you stand beside the bust of Queen Victoria you tell yourself the easy things: it was a long time ago; it has no bearing on my life. But these bring no comfort. The disgust is overpowering. You cannot stop thinking about the men and women he sold on to the ships. You wonder what kind of temperament it took to be a slave trader. And whether the responsibility for his actions runs through your blood. You walk through Kotokuraba market square, past the swirl of street traders and the scent of smoked mackerel. You are full of shame.

On the highway leading out of Cape Coast a sixteen-wheel juggernaut loaded with logs rumbled past me. I covered my face against the dust and carried on walking. According to Albert the town of Pedu lay twenty minutes down the highway. I was on my way to find a cemetery.

In my mind, I see the young Joseph growing up with caramel skin and loose curly hair that he slathers into a parting with coconut oil. He is driven by trade, and the lightness of his skin allied to the name de Graft allows him to move easily between Europeans and Africans. Before long, he has established himself as a Cape Coast slave trader like his father. As Joseph would have understood it, slavery fell into two types.

Down on the shore, with their ships and forts, the Europeans had created an international system of exchange and profit based on the exploitation of human labour. But there was a domestic slave trade that far preceded the international form. For centuries prior to the arrival of Europe, Africans had enslaved Africans. Warring tribes turned captured prisoners into serfs. Families repaid debts by pawning a son or daughter into servitude. With the arrival of the Europeans, the domestic trade became linked to the international system. Mulatto middlemen such as Joseph bought slaves from Africans and sold them to the ships, tightening the links of commerce and complicity until they stretched from the interior of Africa across the Atlantic.

As I walked along the highway, I imagined Joseph visiting Salaga, site of the great market in northern Ghana where merchants gathered from the neighbouring Asante empire, from Hausaland in the north, and from the eastern states of Yoruba and Dahomey. Past the traders squatting before trays of cowrie shells and kola nuts, Joseph would have come to the section of the market where dozens of men and women were roped together for sale. Walked to Salaga by northern traders, they stood naked, the welts of beatings dark on their skin, as merchants such as Joseph bartered over their worth.

The slave business would have offered no struggle of conscience to him. How could it when it was so common-place? Each year 15,000 men and women were sold at Salaga. Most became domestic servants and joined the household of a chief. Owning slaves was a symbol of power. Rich noblemen kept them by the hundred to farm their land, defend their homes and bear their children. In Asante during the eighteenth century, a third of the population was made up of slaves. They provided the army. They worked the fields and the gold mines the state depended on for its wealth. Slaves could be found in the royal household, as stool carriers, drummers, horn blowers, bathroom attendants, hammock carriers, elephant-tail switchers, minstrels and eunuchs.

Under Asante law, a female slave could marry her master or her master's son, and a favoured male slave could wed his master's daughter. Their children would be born free, and it was forbidden for any citizen to disclose the family background of another. Within a few generations, the descendants of slaves could find themselves fully integrated into Asante society.

Slaves could even became part of the nobility. Under the Asante king Osei Bonsu, the palace slave Opuku Frere rose to become Chancellor of the Exchequer in 1800 – an ascension he celebrated by establishing his own household of slaves. The vagaries of the domestic trade threw up other notable figures, not least of whom was John Konny, the 'Negro Prince of Prussia'.

In 1711, Konny, a fifty-year-old African merchant, controlled Cape Three Points, a lucrative trading site on the coast. Its position gave him a local monopoly over commerce. All slaves bought by Europeans, all guns and schnapps and cowrie shells sold to Africans – all business went through Konny. To the chagrin of the Dutch and British castles nearby, Konny preferred to trade with the fort of Great Fredericksburg, which was maintained by the Prussian state of Brandenburg, a minor force in Africa compared to its more powerful European neighours on the coast.

Over the years, Dutch officers in the next-door fort of Axim had watched with alarm as Konny's influence grew. A report to the West India Company dated 16 August 1711 noted that Konny was 'more and more chasing away our subject peoples, robbing some of them, killing others; he has furthermore dared to declare war upon us, threatening to commit similar acts of violence under our fort.' Another report, in 1715, complained of his reluctance to honour an outstanding debt. Konny had offered instead 'flimsy excuses, such as the continuous rainfall, and later, an accident to his arm'.

Konny's power was such, wrote the Governor of Axim castle, that the local people 'admit that they have to bow for him, nay, that they have to give their wives and children to him, if he desires them to do so'.

In December 1716, the Governor of Great Fredericksburg returned to Brandenburg. Konny seized the opportunity to consolidate his strength. Announcing himself its custodian, he took command of the fort, jettisoning the Prussian soldiers and stationing 900 of his own troops in their place. When slave ships from Europe were sighted at Cape Three Points they were greeted with a six-gun salute from the fort's battlements.

Attended by an honour guard of thirty troops and a servant clutching a gold-headed cane engraved with his master's initials, Konny would receive his visitors at the shore and lead them to the fort where a dinner of kenkey and palm wine would be waiting for them in the main hall. Adorned with bracelets and necklaces of pure gold weighing several pounds, Konny would sit at the head of the table and regale his guests in imperfect English richly peppered with expletives.

Determined to drive him from the coast, the West India Company sent a trio of frigates to Cape Three Points in 1718. Under a covering bombardment of fireballs and cannon, 120 soldiers stormed the fort. The attack was a disaster for the Dutch – Konny had been expecting them. His men returned fire from the battlements, killing most of the Dutch as they scrambled up the beach, and forcing the rest into retreat. Afterwards he lined the path to the fort with their skulls. Konny held court at Great Fredericksburg for another seven years until Dutch forces armed with heavy mortars finally destroyed his defences. Even then, they failed to capture him. Eluding his enemies, the Negro Prince of Prussia disappeared into the Asante kingdom, where he remained a free man until his death several years later.

As a consequence of men such as Konny, the practice of slavery was embedded in Ghanaian society. When the British abolished the international trade in 1807, King Osei Bonsu of Asante protested vociferously. 'The white men do not understand my country,' said the king. 'Otherwise they would not say the slave trade was bad.' In light of his protests, domestic slavery was allowed to remain legal in the Gold Coast until 1874.

Is it right to say, I wondered while walking along the highway, that Ghana was built on slavery? States such as Asante and Fante became rich through involvement with the Atlantic trade. Yet whatever short-term profits they made were outweighed by the eventual cost of collusion with Europe: a million Ghanaians shipped across the ocean in the eighteenth century, an enfeebled economy and Britain's colonial takeover in the nineteenth century.

Within the space of an afternoon I felt as if I'd become aged and brittle. I recognized the sensation. It was the same one I'd had when I was eleven years old and coming to realize the implications of the coup; when at seventeen a taxi drove past me with its light on for the first time; and on the first occasion, at the age of twenty, a policeman stopped me in the street and searched my pockets. Each time it seemed as if I'd stepped beyond a veil of idealism to find the realpolitik of a cold world.

Every time it happened I was certain I'd learned the true nature of things. I thought I'd never be gulled into believing in fairness or equality again. It's amazing how tempting it is to cling to those ideals, though. You tell yourself it's a one-off; that the taxi driver was in a hurry or the policeman was just doing his job. Only when different people do the same things over and over do you finally surrender your illusions. Even then, when you assume yourself wiser and more bitter, with a shrunken capacity for hope, even then you will still find yourself horrified by the latest dispatch from the hard frontier.

Before going to Ghana, I was sure the story of the slave trade was one of white brutality and African victimhood. It is true that black people were raped, kidnapped and sold by whites, but that does not mark the limits of the story. Some Africans, such as Joseph de Graft, were collaborators in that dehumanization. To insist otherwise would be to believe that Africans were too meek to resist the European forces landing on their shore. Or too simple-minded to see through the blandishments of white traders.

Coercion and seduction took place. But Africans also sold Africans by choice; because they stood to gain from it. For centuries they'd practised a trade between themselves that was similar to serfdom. Perhaps, when the Europeans arrived, they imagined that Atlantic slavery was just an extension of that system. If that was the case they couldn't have been more mistaken.

The advent of white people introduced the ideology of race to slavery. Europe justified its brutality on the basis of its 'natural' superiority to black people. In doing so, they set in place a notion of genetic inequality that still remains central to white self-belief.

This is where my ancestor was most culpable. The mulatto Joseph de Graft exploited his white parentage to do business with the forts. The lightness of his skin and his Dutch surname enabled him to turn the European belief in African savagery into an advantage over his local black rivals. In this he wasn't alone. By the close of the eighteenth century, some 800 mulattoes lived around the European trading posts. Many were employed as servants at the forts. Others were independently wealthy, such as Jan Neiser of Elmina, a rich and influential merchant contemporary of Joseph de Graft, with a declared contempt for 'stupid blacks'.

You imagine that the events of history take place in some nebulous 'other time' unrelated to your own life. Yet I feel the consequences of Joseph's actions every day in Britain. It was partly because of the pervasiveness of racism there that I'd come to Ghana – only to find my ancestor had collaborated in establishing its tenets.

At such moments you yearn to stand back and reflect on the ironies of history. In reality it's impossible to find the distance. The shock is physical. You feel winded. The sun is too bright. Your head aches. You find yourself walking along a sand-blown highway no longer sure who you are any more.

IV

There were thirty gravestones, leaning away from each other at precarious angles in the grass. From the highway I'd turned off into Pedu and found my way to the small, overgrown cemetery. I'd scoured foliage from the head-stones of a dozen faithful husbands and dearly departed mothers before I discovered the grave for which I was searching. I traced the inscription with my hand:

Joseph de Graft, Nobleman, Merchant, Warrior, Statesman, Patriot
And then, in Latin:
Acta Non Verba (Action not words) 1756–1840

Deep down I'd wanted to dismiss Albert's story about Joseph as an old man's yarn. But he was here memorialized in stone. The fact of his existence stared back at me so baldly that, overcome with a sudden light-headedness, I had to sit down with my back to the gravestone to recover myself.

For Joseph, the slave trade brought rapid wealth. Near the British-owned Cape Coast castle he built a mansion, with a basement specially designed to pen his slaves before they were sold abroad.

Riches lent him the status of a chief. When Cape Coast came under attack from the Asante he donated 800 ounces of gold towards the maintenance of British troops at the castle. In 1824 he raised a private army of 300 men to join the British counterinvasion of Asante territory. The battle went badly. British forces were overrun at the river Pra. Their commander, Sir Charles McCarthy, was beheaded. Joseph managed to escape the rout and return to Cape Coast. After the battle he eschewed fighting for business.

He bought virgin land at Pedu and allowed the hardest-working slaves to settle there in their own homes instead of being shipped away. Joseph's slaves came from all over Ghana. Captured at war or kidnapped from their homes, they arrived separated from their families, and speaking little Fante. In Pedu they became part of his household. Even after the British abolition of the international trade he continued to keep bonded labour. Two of his five wives were Pedu slaves. Their children were free-born, the distinction between slaves and extended family becoming increasingly indistinguishable as the household grew.

Shielding my face from the sun, I got to my feet and searched the rest of the headstones for Joseph's brother William. There was no sign of him, which seemed appropriate. From the little I knew about him, I suspected they must have been quite different. William was an ordained Methodist minister, one of the founders of the Church in Ghana. He travelled the country preaching, and I imagine that what he saw along the way made him question the morality of Joseph's wealth.

In the westerly Akwamu region William would have heard tales of the 'Sicca Dingers', kidnap gangs who raided villages at night and sold their captives as slaves. He would have crossed through neighbouring states spurred into conflict by the high price that prisoners of war fetched on the coast. He'd have seen villages in the north stripped bare by slave raiders, and fertile land lying fallow because there was no one left to cultivate it. In Asante, he'd have come across innocent people facing fraudulent claims of theft or adultery because the penalty of guilt was enslavement to the accuser. He would have realized that the whole country was devouring itself for the sake of the Atlantic trade. And he would probably have agreed with the findings of a Dutch West India Company report from 1730:

The part of Africa which as of old is known as the 'Gold Coast' . . . has now virtually changed into a pure Slave Coast; the great quantity of guns and powder which the Europeans have brought there has given cause to terrible wars among the Kings, Princes and Caboceers of those lands, who made their prisoners of war slaves; these slaves were immediately bought up by the Europeans at steadily increasing prices, which in turn animated again and again those people to renew their hostilities, and their hope for big and easy profits made them forget all labour, using all sorts of pretexts to attack each other, or reviving old disputes. Consequently, there is now very little trade among the coast Negroes except in slaves.

Yet William would have been a brave man to reveal any such misgivings to his brother. In Asante, Swiss Methodist missionaries had been executed for calling for an end to slavery. William would probably have kept his own counsel. When Joseph died at eighty-four and William delivered the funeral oration, he no doubt spoke of his brother's courage and generosity. I wonder, though, if in solitude William believed that nothing good could come of Joseph's wealth?

*

'When Joseph bought the land at Pedu it was just forest, it was his slaves that cleared it,' Nana Banyin had said earlier that afternoon. 'After his death they carried on living there. In the years since then Pedu has grown from a settlement into a proper town with homes and offices and government buildings. The descendants of Joseph's original slaves are still living there. They claim Pedu belongs to them. They've been selling off the land in their name. We, the de Graft Johnson family, are fighting them in court. Joseph bought the land. It belongs to us. Unfortunately the original deeds have been lost over the years. It's hard for us to prove ownership. If we win then Joseph's legacy comes to us. We'll be rich.'

Nana Banyin pushed himself out of his chair. He shuffled down the corridor and returned with a tan leather satchel. From the satchel he pulled out the minutes of court proceedings, appeals, adjournments and other legal documents, all of them embossed with official seals in blood-red wax. Leafing through them I realized the case between the de Graft Johnson family and the descendants of the Pedu slaves had been going on in court for the past three decades and still showed no sign of resolution. All of the family members who'd started the legal battle were now dead – the last in the previous year.

'He died alone in his room,' said Nana Banyin. 'Everyone thought he'd gone to Accra and locked his room behind him. It was only after a week we noticed the smell. His body was so swollen it wouldn't fit through the door. We had to wrap it in a rug and lift it through the window.

Now there's only me left to chase the case and I'm not so young, as you see.'

He looked up from the papers. There was something in the slow unfurling of his neck and the heaviness of his gaze. Was Nana Banyin sizing me up to take over the case? A bead of sweat rolled down my back. I noticed that we were both holding the same court report from opposite ends. Outside a rook cawed.

Abruptly, Nana Banyin stuffed the papers back into the satchel and walked down the corridor without a word. At the end of the hall down which he'd disappeared, I pictured a back room with shelves piled with yellowed legal papers. This was how Joseph's legacy ended. Not in *acta*, but *verba*. Words rising in columns of paper, collapsing to dust even as they grew towards the ceiling.

V

What did Joseph's life tell me about mine? Only that there is no singularity to truth. He was a slave trader who sold Africans. He was a soldier who defended his town. A landowner and a patrician. None of these descriptions cancels the others out. They simply make for a disorderly whole.

The day after I learned about Joseph a lump about the size of a marble materialized under my right eyelid. It didn't hurt, but it forced my eye shut and gave me the look of a boxer who'd gone down in the third without much of a struggle. Peering half-blind into my hotel-room mirror I looked for signs of an insect bite or an allergic rash. Nothing. The lump was tender to the touch, but otherwise painless. I concluded its cause was mental, not physical. It seemed significant that I'd lost vision in one eye. My body was staging a protest at the dualities I'd found in Ghana. Enough of ambiguity, it said. Give it to me straight.

For centuries Europeans had been coming to Africa imagining it as a place of primal honesty. Through their accounts of journeying along the Congo, the Nile and other rivers, Victorian explorers such as Livingstone and Stanley invented the notion of the Dark Continent with its savage tribes and impenetrable jungle. How many of those myths had I absorbed growing up in London? Blindness showed me what my mind refused to accept. That complexity scared me. This was my fear: if I was Joseph's descendant did that make me tainted by his actions?

I pressed at the lump. Yet it seemed to me that I'd spent my life paying the cost of Joseph's profits. Slavery is impossible to forget if you are born in Britain. It is present in galleries such as Tate Britain and in Bristol's Theatre Royal, both of which were built from Caribbean sugar money. It is remembered by the streets of Liverpool named after eighteenth-century plantation aristocrats, such as Earle Street, Cunliffe Street and Bold Street. And it lives in the collective memory of the black people who have arrived in Britain since the mass immigrations of the 1950s. What is it that keeps us going against the daily fact of prejudice? Why don't we just go 'home'? Perhaps because we see life through two eyes. We see possibility as well as prejudice. We see the miscegenation of things – black crossing over with white; wrong ameliorated by right.

Maybe over time all the world's crimes balance out. For each indolent Horace there is a hard-working Robert Newton. For every Joseph a William. Cape Coast itself, I thought, squinting into the mirror, is hardly a town of singular truths. It is the home of families with names such as de Graft Johnson, Hutton Brew and Casley Hayford. Of Cruickshanks, Van Heins, Brownwells, Mountfords, Butlers and Edmundsons. Names that originated in London, Amsterdam, Copenhagen and The Hague.

Even in Africa everyone comes from somewhere else.

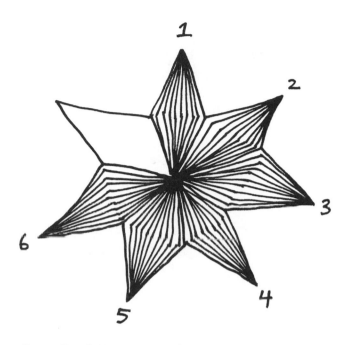

Busua Beach Resort – Drinking at Zion – Big Men and Small Boys – Mr Prempeh returns to Kumasi – The sermon of Bishop Maxwell-Smith – The mysterious death of Richard Wright – Pursued by nightmares – The face of my killer

I

I was worn out. I needed a break. I caught a tro-tro from Cape Coast and rode west along the highway towards the beach village of Busua, which according to my guide book was 'a great place to chill out for a few days'.

Squeezed into the back I nodded off to sleep by the window and woke up a few hours later to find the bus had turned off the highway and was huffing its way up a dirt track, dodging the minor crevasses in its way. Each time it came to a stop at one of the villages by the roadside, local women clamoured round the windows selling boiled eggs and mugs of cocoa, and loaves of hot kenkey wrapped in banana leaves. I bought a plastic bag filled with iced water and watched fields of red earth undulate beyond the window until the tro-tro finally shuddered to a halt at Busua.

The village had one street and plenty of goats. Shop-keepers were still rubbing the sleep out of their eyes. It was five o'clock in the afternoon.

I followed the street round the corner and came to the entrance of the Busua Beach Resort hotel. A pair of security guards flipped their noses up at me as I passed through the gates. Inside, rows of chalets stood on tended lawns. Gardeners clipped at immaculate hedges. Waiters in white gloves pushed serving trolleys along the pathways. I crossed an acreage of grass. The lobby doors whooshed apart. My footsteps echoed across the marble tiles.

'I'd like your least expensive room, please.'

The receptionist was as well groomed as the lawn. As she looked up, I became conscious that somewhere between Cape Coast and Busua I'd acquired a fine layering of dust over my face and clothes. Her tone was cooler than the lobby's glacial air conditioning.

'Normally we are fully booked well in advance. But we do have a budget room available. You'll have to pay in dollars. In advance.'

'No problem,' I said, trying to muster a jaunty air.

A bellboy led me out past the chalets.

'Where are you from? he said.

'London. Well, actually, my family's from Cape Coast.'

'Wofra wo den?' he asked in Fante.

'Ekow.'

'Eh-*kor*, Akwaba. You are most welcome, my brother. I'm Kwame.'

He gave me a sidelong look and started laughing.

'What's so funny?' I said.

'When you walked into the lobby we thought you were from Ghana. We get guests who come here from Takoradi and Accra. They think they are big men. If they've been to Yankee they put on a new voice to go with their new clothes. *Wobo life papa* – they put on the style!

'Eh, my brother, you should see them. They think they are too fine. So when we saw you, we said to ourselves, you must be one of them.'

Kwame led me towards the distant perimeter of the hotel, past the staff canteen, the hotel laundry and the enormous galvanized steel bins where vultures picked at the rubbish, until we came to a strip of breezeblock rooms with battered screen doors.

'We only have a double left, but for you, my brother,

I'll see you're charged the price for one person,' he said, opening the door on to a spare, clean room with a view out over the beach.

'This will do fine,' I said.

Kwame gave me a vigorous slap on the back and left shaking his head, apparently overcome with hilarity at my presence.

I stayed at Busua for a week. Joseph de Graft often floated into my thoughts. Each time I tried to figure out his life I felt the same sensation of horror, like the moment when the cars reach the highest point on a roller-coaster ride and sit teetering on the edge of oblivion.

I spent the week lying on the beach and swimming out into the high Atlantic waves. Even when the riptide took me and I was dragged round and round beneath the surface of the water Joseph was on my mind. I must have looked quite melancholy wandering the Beach Resort grounds on my own because, largely due to Kwame I suspect, the staff adopted me as the hotel mascot.

Over breakfast, Ralph and Ato, the waiters, would crouch by my table. 'You have the cash and we have the connections, my brother. We can't fail!' they'd say, trying to convince me to back their putative bush-meat export business. At the gates, the security guards now gave a jaunty salute each time I passed. Even Madame, the fearsome matriarch in charge of housekeeping, looked kindly on me. Whenever I passed her small, neat office, she'd call me in and make me speak to her in Fante so that, as she put it, I could learn to become a real Ghanaian.

In its own way, staying at the hotel was as disorienting as trying to negotiate through Accra had been when I first arrived. In the extremity of its orderliness – its cultivated lawns and sweet-scented flower bushes – the Beach Resort was the antithesis of the bustling streets I'd come to think of as authentically Ghanaian. Faced with the friendliness of Kwame, Madame and the rest of the staff, I felt some of my defensiveness begin to evaporate. I'd become used to thinking of myself as a stranger in Ghana, but it occurred to me now that finding a sense of belonging might involve no greater mystery than allowing yourself to accept a place in all its idiosyncrasy. Being Ghanaian was not just a matter of whose genes you had, I told myself at those moments. It could also be an act of voluntarism. If you made the effort you could even discover a home among strangers.

'Everyone in the village is talking about you.'

I was having a drink outside the hotel, at a bar on the beach, when a young Ghanaian with shoulder-length dreadlocks sat down beside me.

'You spend all day on your own and you stay in the Beach Resort where everything is so expensive,' he said. 'They say you must be a black American with too much money.'

'It costs me $10 a night for the budget room. I stay there because it's clean and quiet.'

'Compared to the rest of us then, you *are* rich. When

the people see you coming down the street they call you Burenyi.'

He started to laugh, but stopped when he noticed the look of dismay on my face.

'Don't worry. Everyone talks in this village. There's nothing else to do. It was the same when I first came here.'

He said his name was Daniel and that he'd grown up in the Volta region, in the east of Ghana.

'If you grow locks in Ghana people think you are a bad person. The neighbours said I was a thief. It was a lie, but my parents threw me out. For the past few years I've just been travelling around Africa by myself.'

Daniel told me how he'd hitched a ride with a lorry driver across the Sahara the previous year.

'There was me and two Arab guys on our way through the desert to Bamako, in Mali. Halfway across, the driver stops the truck. He makes us get out and stand in the sand.

'"Give me all your money or I leave you here," he says.

'The Arab guys are scared. We hand over our money. Then he starts the truck and drives off. We chase after him, but the truck goes off fast.

'Now we're alone. We start following the tyre tracks. The sand is shifting under our feet. It feels like we're not moving. We don't have much water, and the wind starts to whine like an aeroplane. It picks up the sand and sends it whirling around us. We're caught in a sandstorm.

'We can't tell if we're going in the right direction. Our eyes are stinging. We're thirsty and frightened. One of the

Arab guys sits down. He's crying. His friend is pulling him up but he says he can't go on.'

'What did you do?'

'We have to leave him there, otherwise we'll all die. At least if we go ahead we can find help. We walk through the storm until we reach a small town. The police listen to our story. Then they try to arrest us. They say we must have tried to hold up the driver. The Arab guy is shouting about his friend. But they want to arrest us. We manage to slip away, and I grabbed another lift and got out of town, otherwise I'd probably still be there.'

Daniel traced a pattern in the sand with his toe.

'After that, I don't worry so much about anything. Each time I arrive at a new place I remember the desert and that wind and I thank Jah for still keeping me on this earth. That's why, when I saw you on your own, I said I must talk to this person.'

We sat at the bar drinking and talking through the afternoon until, with sunset, Daniel took me to Zion, a reggae bar arranged under a canopy of palm trees at the far end of Busua beach.

'That's Ocean,' he said, nodding at a young dread behind the bar. 'He comes from Kumasi, but he had to leave home when he started growing locks, so he came down here, saved up some money and opened this place.'

'It not be much, true,' said Ocean, joining us. 'But this bar be righteous place for good people. Yes iya, so just relax and be cool.'

He rolled a joint and we smoked it without speaking. A

string of fairy lights hung from the palm fronds, and beyond them I could make out the glimmer of the stars. Over the speakers Horace Andy pleaded a love song into the warm night. The surf uncoiled itself on to the beach in silvery threads.

By the time the joint's effect had worn off, Zion was full of white backpackers, Ghanaian dreads and local kids attracted by the thump of the music and the buzz of conversation. A fire-eater juggled burning clubs, there was dancing beneath the palms and, every so often, a group of backpackers would run squealing with laughter into the sea, then trek back up to the bar, dripping wet, voices ringing with exhilaration.

Later in the night, in an advanced state of deterioration, I discovered myself in conversation with a young dread who called himself Black Prophet.

'Me, I never read no book apart from the Bible,' he was telling me. 'White man say human being dem come from monkeys. But me know this is lie. The only truth be Jah. He build the heaven and the earth as it say in the Bible.'

There followed a lengthy critique of evolutionism during which Black Prophet produced a pocket-sized Bible and began to read from Genesis in a forthright tone. Somewhere around chapter 6, verse 5 ('Then the Lord said the wickedness of man was great in the earth'), I made my escape and found Daniel.

'Why do all the dreads here have Jamaican accents?' I asked.

'They want to be true Rastafari, so they try to speak like

they were born in the Blue Mountains,' he said. 'The senior guys like Ocean are cool, but some of the young ones like your friend Black Prophet – all they know is Jah, Jah, Jah. To find answers you have to ask questions, but all they want to do is tell you what to think.'

'You know what's funny about this place?' I said, watching the lights in the palm trees wink red, gold and green. 'Everyone here is looking for something. If you're Black Prophet, you put on a Jamaican accent even though you were born in Accra. If you're a white backpacker you braid your hair and take drumming lessons because you think that brings you closer to the real Africa. But most Ghanaians go home after work, watch *The Cosby Show* and dream about living in America. Everyone's searching for a reality that doesn't exist.'

Daniel rolled a bottle of beer between his palms.

'What about you?' he said. 'What are you looking for?'

'I don't know. Nothing here is what I expected. It's like, you think you're going to find your roots, but all you end up with is this tangled mess.'

I wanted to tell him about Joseph de Graft. It could be that he'd have a similar story to tell, in return. Whose roots in Ghana *didn't* reach back into the slave trade, after all? But the thought of Joseph filled me with shame. I felt like an outsider   a Burenyi – and I wondered if the sensation would ever go away.

I waved goodbye to Daniel and walked down the beach towards the lights of the Beach Resort.

*

Saturday in Busua. The chalets fill up with businessmen on a weekend break from Takoradi, the nearest big city. They swagger round the hotel, bellies preceding them, and a mistress on their arm. Watching them I remember a night shortly after I arrived in Accra. I was out with Kobby, my cousin, when a policeman pulled over his car. We were speeding and one of our rear lights was out, he said, opening his book to write us a ticket.

'Please, mepa wo kyeo, I will fix the light tomorrow,' said Kobby. 'I know I did wrong. Master, I beg you.'

The policeman tried to frown. But his lips flickered upward in rebellion. He started on a lecture about traffic observance that gave way to a protracted homily on respecting your betters.

'OK, you can go,' he said finally. 'But remember I will know your car and if I stop it again I will not be so kind. Don't let me see you again.'

We drove off in silence. I stared out of the window, embarrassed by Kobby's fawning and confused by the policeman's reaction. Kobby seemed to be enjoying my discomfort.

'So, you see how we handle things in Ghana?' he said. 'All he wanted was to be treated like a "Big Man". Doing that cost me nothing. In fact it saved me something because I didn't get a fine. This is the Ghanaian way. You have to realize that a lot of those guys – police officers, army men, bank managers – don't get paid very much. All they have is respect. That's what it means to be a Big Man. Everyone looks up to you. So if you make them feel important, they'll be generous back to you. Think about it. He stopped me because I broke the law. But I was the one who made him do what I wanted.'

According to Kobby, it was the Big Men who ran Ghana. They were the politicians, doctors and lawyers, whose work gave them an elevated status in the community. To be a true Big Man had less to do with occupation than attitude, though. They carried themselves with a bluffness that reminded me of nineteenth-century mill owners. All afternoon, for instance, the Takoradi businessmen had been barking orders at Kwame and the other hotel staff. Over lunch, I'd seen one of them actually snap his fingers for service. Determined to announce their superiority to ordinary Ghanaians, everything about them spoke of superciliousness, from their stentorian voices to the expanse of their bellies.

A few days later I took a bus to Takoradi to change some money. It had been raining all morning. By the time I got to the bank the water was running freely off my clothes. I squelched across the floor to join the queue. As I did so, the manager rushed out of his office towards me.

'You there! Yes, you there,' he said. 'What do you think you're doing?'

He pointed at the trail of water behind me.

'Is this how you treat your own home? Clean it up! Get on your knees and clean it up!'

Men and women in the queue turned to stare. Bank

clerks froze in the middle of stamping cheques. The whirr of a ceiling fan became violently audible.

I'd come face to face with a Big Man.

'Are you deaf?' he asked. 'I told you to clean it up! Why do you still stand there?'

No one had spoken to me that way since I was a child. According to Kobby I could retain my dignity by begging the manager for mercy. By the same logic, though, I'd win an even better victory by getting to my knees and cleaning the floor.

I couldn't bring myself to do it.

'Clean your own floor,' I said. 'I'm sorry if it's wet, but you may have noticed it's raining outside. If you want it dry do it yourself. Otherwise, leave me alone!'

For a moment, as the manager stood paralysed by his own fury, I found myself studying the line of sweat that ran from the crown of his balding head to the ridge of his eyebrows. I noticed the orange specks of palm nut soup on his white shirt and how the fifth button had popped loose under pressure from his stomach. Then he began to roar again.

'Who are you?' he said. 'How dare you speak to me like this?'

'I told you I'm sorry, but I'm not going to clean it. I'm not here for a fight. All I want to do is cash some travellers cheques.'

His eyes narrowed.

I could see the calculations working behind them.

My accent wasn't Ghanaian.

I had travellers cheques.

The pieces fell together.

An unctuous smile glazed his face.

'I can tell from your voice you're not from here,' he said. 'Why didn't you say so to begin with. We have to be very careful with the people who come into this bank. Some of them are just here to waste our time. Please, come with me. I'll see you're not detained any longer.'

Taking me by the elbow he steered me past the other customers to the front of the queue.

'If there's anything else I can do after you're finished here, please come and see me.'

Half bowing, the manager retreated to his office and shut himself in.

I passed my travellers cheques to the cashier without meeting her eyes. What had happened? My status as a westerner had superseded his position as a provincial bank manager. Once he realized he was outranked, he'd taken the Kobby option and backed down.

The entire argument left me disgusted. I hurried out of the bank with my cash and ordered a bottle of Coke at a bar across the road. I pictured the manager's face as it shifted from anger to obsequiousness. Then I imagined how haughty I must have looked in return. Westerners had been behaving with assumed superiority since they first came to Africa. It hurt to find myself acting the same way.

True, the manager deserved it. But Ghana already had enough Big Men without me joining them.

I drained my Coke and sat watching the traffic go by outside the bar.

It occurred to me that for every Big Man there must also be a Small Boy – the victim of authority who, unlike me, had no power of his own with which to retaliate. The following afternoon brought proof of his existence. At Takoradi passport office, I witnessed an argument between a clerk and a young man as I waited to renew my visa.

The young man said he'd picked up his passport yesterday, but when he'd got home he realized he'd been given the wrong one. The clerk snatched the passport from him and flicked through it with pursed lips.

'Are you telling me you're not Kwaku Paulson, occupation carpenter?'

'Yes, boss, that's me.'

'Then why are you wasting our time? Can't you see we're busy?'

'But the picture is wrong. It's my name. But you've put the wrong man's photo in my passport.'

The clerk glared at the young man.

'We can't be held responsible if you don't check your documents before picking them up. You should have been more careful. Do you know how many Kwaku Paulsons we have to deal with in this office?'

He gestured vaguely behind him, suggesting the presence of a mountainous heap of passports all marked 'Kwaku Paulson'.

'We can't be expected to do our job with people like

you around. If you're so careless what do you want us to do?'

Kwaku Paulson's head sunk into his shoulders like a rain-soaked bird.

'How can I travel with an incorrect passport? Please, master, I have to go to Germany next week.'

The clerk held the picture up to the light.

'All the details in here are correct, yes?'

Kwaku Paulson nodded.

'It's only a matter of the picture?'

Kwaku Paulson agreed that was the case.

'Then I don't see we have a problem after all,' said the clerk triumphantly. 'When you look at it, the photo isn't very far off from you. It's really a very good match.'

His fellow clerks gathered round and scrutinized the picture. One of them gave it to an elderly woman standing at the counter. She passed it down the queue for further examination. Consensus among her fellow customers had it that the photo was a good likeness. The only dissenter was Kwaku Paulson.

'Please, master, I have a young family. If I go to Germany with this passport they will deport me. I beg you.'

The clerk summoned an especially severe expression.

'Look, just because this is a passport office you can't think you have the right to automatically receive your passport. We're not miracle workers. Just this once we'll issue a new passport. We won't even charge you. How's that?'

Overcome by his own magnanimity, the clerk held out his hand. Kwaku Paulson shook it limply.

'Even the best of us makes mistakes sometimes,' said the clerk. 'Let that be a lesson to you.'

On the bus back to Busua, I replayed what I'd seen in the past few days. If I could, I'd have gathered all the Big Men in Ghana, along with the Small Boys they preyed on, taken them to London, and shown them the relativity of power. We could have waited on a street corner trying to hail a taxi while the cab drivers rolled by with their lights on. I'd have pointed out the bags drawn closer to legs when we boarded the tube; the white women who crossed the road when we were walking down the street behind them; the receptionist's confusion when we arrived at an office and proved not to be a courier.

And then I'd have asked them why we were struggling to put distance between ourselves in Ghana when the whole of the west was ready to do it for us? Maybe it was a naive question that failed to take into account all the nuances of class, income and tradition in Ghanaian society. Even so, I'd have liked an answer.

The following evening I left Busua. At Takoradi station, I booked a berth on the sleeper to Kumasi. The train pulled out into the falling light. Past the windows the giant machines of bauxite mines were rendered infernal by the darkness, as if they were boring a way to the underworld. All through the night I rode away from the sea. Yet the further I left it behind the more clearly I heard its emanations: the bubblings of a submerged volcano; the soundings of whales calling over fantastic distance; a continental shelf groaning at the centuries of civilization that rose from its back, unaware of their accumulated mass.

II

The ghost of Joseph de Graft walked next to me in Kumasi. The thought of him stripped away the pleasure of finding myself in a new place. I wandered the city aimlessly, beset by a gloominess it seemed impossible to shift. At the central market I watched a butcher drive his knife up the belly of a dead goat and strip the corpse clean out of its skin. At Lake Bosumtwi I lay on my back and tried to imitate the passivity of the jellyfish as it is borne across the surface of the ocean.

I visited the Manhiya Palace, home to the Asante king Prempeh I in the 1920s. It was a place of advanced melancholy. In the king's old office, with its bakelite phone and leather-covered desk top, moths fluttered irritably through shafts of afternoon sunlight before settling back among manila files to lay their eggs. A spider had spun a web over a waxwork of the Asante queen mother Yaa Awantwa. It hovered before her face like a veil. Amid the relics and waxworks of the palace, my spirits dipped further.

In 1896, following the British overthrow of the Asante empire, Prempeh was stripped of his title and exiled to the Seychelles, aged twenty-six. Twenty-eight years later he was allowed to return to Kumasi as plain Mr Prempeh. Little is recorded of his time away, although a photograph exists of the former king on the forward deck of a ship, as it departed Liverpool for the final leg of his return voyage to the Gold Coast. Prempeh is hunched inside his coat, and the foretaste of homecoming and bitterness of exile mingle in his gaze.

Wandering through Kumasi, I felt as lost as the deposed king. In the heat of the afternoon, the ground seemed to pitch like the deck of a ship.

I went to church that Sunday. Curiosity took me there rather than faith. Ghana, along with most of West Africa, was in the midst of a boom in charismatic Christian churches – the kind that boasted spectacular acts of miracle working and faith healing. Most of them seemed to be in Kumasi. Next door to my hotel, the Higher Ground Faith Ministries held all-night prayer sessions that shook me awake in the early hours as the congregation's singing and speaking in tongues reached their fervid pitch. On television preachers hollered like showmen, lifting their arms to heaven and slamming their Bibles on the lectern until their flock began to shake and howl and fall to the floor. Itinerant pastors stood on street corners haranguing passers-by through megaphones with gothic descriptions of hell. Shops bore names such as God is Able Plumbing Works; Shine, Jesus, Shine Fashion Centre; Omnipotent God Spare Parts; and – my personal favourite – Humble Yourself Bicycle Repairing. The churches ranged from shopfront chapels to stadium-sized arenas. Outside them you might find a list of services offered, including prophesying, deliverance from demonic possession, faith healing through prayers, laying on of hands, telepathy, visions and 'remote control'.

I decided to visit one of the largest churches in Ghana. The Holy Power Faith Chapel was founded by Bishop David Maxwell-Smith, the flashiest of the showmen preachers. He owned a fleet of American cars, a mansion in Accra and a family home in Washington DC from where he flew first class every weekend to deliver a sermon at one of the 150 branches of his church in Ghana.

His largest chapel in Accra held 3,000 people. The Kumasi outpost, at the edge of the city, looked as if it might do the same when it was completed. Although it was open the building work hadn't finished, and when I arrived I took a seat at the back near the scaffolding that covered the rear wall. Despite this, the rows of folding chairs leading down to the stage were full. A warm-up preacher was addressing the congregation accompanied by a backing band. Each time he made a point, a chorus of 'Hallelujah's and 'Praise God's rose from the crowd.

Seated on a red velvet throne at the side of the stage, Maxwell-Smith wore a purple three-piece suit and a goatee beard. When he stood, the band fell silent and the audience seemed to hold its collective breath.

The bishop pointed to the bare walls. By the time the church was complete, he said, it would hold a crèche, a computer room, a swimming pool for baptisms and 'the finest car park in Ghana'.

Beneath the beam of a spotlight, Maxwell-Smith bowed

his head. To finish construction he was asking that morning for a sacrifice.

'I need you to give some special oils today,' he said.

The bishop raised his eyes.

He looked at the faces of the crowd.

He held out his arms towards them.

'Dearly beloved, this is God speaking through me,' he said. 'To complete this church, I'm asking for a hundred people to step forward and pledge a thousand dollars right now.'

I couldn't believe what I'd heard. The average Ghanaian monthly wage was around 300,000 cedis, or roughly $50. He wanted twenty times that sum in a single cheque. But a few men and women were already heading to the front, the audience applauding as they walked down the aisle.

Surrounded by his aides, Maxwell-Smith descended from the stage and began to walk among the congregation with a radio mike.

'If you can't give $1,000, give $500,' he said.

He passed close enough for me to see his manicured fingernails and the jewelled cross hanging outside his waistcoat.

'It could be the money you've saved to travel: release it!' he said. 'We all have some reserves for a rainy day. It could be your car. Take the keys and sell it! If not $500, then $250.'

He continued halving the amount as he shook hands with members of the congregation. At each drop in price more people rushed down the aisle, waving tithing envelopes. Pushing back through them Maxwell-Smith returned to the stage.

'Dearly beloved. Something wonderful is about to happen.'

Everyone seemed to know what to expect. His voice was barely audible above the cheers.

'The lady who is facing an operation next week – it shall no longer take place. You are better. We are here to witness the working of miracles. The gentleman with the court case – the judgement will go in your favour. The woman who's waiting to hear from her husband – I just got a message from God. It's time for you to join him in America.'

As he scattered his favours, Maxwell-Smith continued calling for more donations. Waving envelopes and cash in the air, men and women ran down the aisle. A scrum formed in front of the stage. I saw women weeping. Others fell to the floor, convulsing. A smartly dressed man in his forties began to babble uncontrollably. More of the throng started speaking in tongues.

I decided I'd seen enough. Head reeling, I hurried outside and climbed on to the first bus I could find that would take me away from the proposed site of the finest car park in Ghana. I felt drained by what I'd seen. Between the Big Men and the preachers I didn't know what to make of the country any more. The longer I stayed, the less sure I was of why I had come.

III

Returning to the centre of Kumasi, I ordered lunch in a restaurant and read about Richard Wright.

Browsing through a second-hand bookstall the previous day I'd discovered a copy of *Black Power*, Wright's account of his journey round the Gold Coast in 1953. Almost fifty years later, Ghana remained entirely recognizable from his description of its noisy, jostling streets. My order of jollof and fried fish arrived. As I studied the book I was struck by the sense of foreboding that had come over Wright as he travelled. Kumasi central market, he wrote, was 'a maelstrom of men and women and children and vultures and mud and stagnant water and flies and filth and foul odours'. Nothing appeared safe to him. After a dinner of fufu and palm nut soup left him sick he suspected poisoning. In the embrace of a chief he sensed malevolence. By the final stages of his journey he'd become obsessed by intimations of his own death. At a funeral, he was chased away by a group of mourners waving machetes and became so frightened for his life that he fled the city and, soon after, the country.

Given the confusions of my own trip I had nothing but sympathy for Wright. But I also suspected there was more to his anxiety than dealing with a strange country.

'Some hovering mystery, some lurking and nameless danger lay amongst its trees,' he wrote of Kumasi. But Wright's fear ran deeper than he admitted. I was sure of it. And the answer might mean something for me, similarly becalmed in Kumasi. Searching my memory I tried to piece together everything I knew about Wright.

The child of Mississippi sharecroppers, Wright was born in 1908 and saw his first novel, *Native Son*, published in 1940. It was an international sensation. Critics compared him to Dostoyevsky and Dickens. The most successful African-American author in history, he left New York for an opulent home in Paris, where he was fêted by Sartre and the writers of the Left Bank.

By the time of his trip to Ghana, however, Wright's fortunes had declined. Book sales were faltering. On returning from Africa, he suffered debilitating bouts of amoebic dysentery. Publishers rejected his manuscripts. His wife left him. Short of money he was forced to move to a smaller apartment.

Alone in Paris he fell to brooding. He became convinced he was the target of a plot involving the CIA, the FBI and the State Department. They were out to destroy his career in revenge for the criticisms he'd published of US foreign policy. At night he slept with a pistol beside his bed.

'I don't want anything to happen to me, but if it does my friends will know exactly where it comes from,' he wrote to a friend in 1960. On 26 November of the same year he was admitted to the Eugene Gibez Clinic in Paris complaining of stomach pains. Two days later he died of a heart attack, aged fifty-two.

With no history of coronary illness, Wright's death was

mysterious. State Department documents released after his passing establish that he really was under surveillance by the secret services. Friends speculated that government agents may have assassinated him with *Rauwolfia serpentina*. A drug known to be favoured by the CIA during the Cold War, it mimics the effects of a heart attack with lethal consequences.

Yet sitting in the restaurant pondering his fate it came to me that the cause of Wright's death was probably more ordinary and terrible than murder.

In my mid twenties, I began suffering from severe nightmares. I'd keep the radio turned on and blinds open to ward off the night, but at some point I'd falter and the dreams would come.

In the gloaming of an underpass, a teenage gang kicked me to the ground. On a rooftop, an assassin hefted his rifle and aimed at my head. From the doorways of a rural town, a crowd coalesced. Wordlessly, they chased me across a square, waving clubs. Sometimes I woke before they caught me. When I didn't they raised their clubs and beat me till I stopped moving.

The dreams came with such force that they began to seem more real than the daytime. I was living in a flat overlooking Upper Street in Islington at the time. The music and laughter from the bars strung along the pavement would rise to my window every evening. There is a righteous anger that can descend on you when the rest of humanity appears oblivious to your distress. You want to smash faces. You want to see blood. You want to spray the street with a machine gun. You want to make them hurt like you do.

After working freelance since leaving LSE, I'd taken a job as an editor on *The Face* magazine. It was only when I was at my desk scrutinizing copy that I was free of the shadow cast by the dreams.

As a result I took to working past midnight.

I turned up at the office on my days off.

I came in over Christmas.

I'd do anything so that I wouldn't have to stay home by myself replaying the events of the previous night.

The dreams persisted. They formed into a recognizable sequence of events: a sniper would stalk me from the rooftops; his face remained hidden; his shots always missed. But I sensed he was getting closer.

Eventually I had a dream where he caught me. He stood over me with a pistol, and I lay on the ground looking up into the muzzle of his gun. We stared at each other in silence, the gun in his hand and the ground beneath me. He pulled the trigger.

I woke up screaming. He had killed me – but not before I'd seen his face.

I ordered a glass of iced water in the restaurant. The memory of those dreams had returned to me as I read through Wright's book. As I turned those scenes over in my mind, I started looking at his life through them.

The horrors I'd encountered took place only in my head.

By comparison Wright's nightmares were real. As a child he'd lived briefly in Arkansas. His family was forced to flee town after Wright's Uncle Hoskins went to work one morning and never returned. He'd been lynched by white farmers. The family escaped in the back of a covered wagon the same day, too frightened to even stage a funeral for Hoskins.

From Arkansas they settled on the south side of Chicago. Wright saw how the indignities of racism led his neighbours to drink and violence and self-loathing. Working in a hotel as a teenager, he met Shorty, the elevator boy. For a quarter Shorty would bend over and let the white guests kick him in the ass. 'This monkey's got the peanuts,' Shorty would bellow as he scrabbled to pick up the coins they'd thrown on the floor.

For all his later success, Wright was never able to leave the brutality of those years behind. He failed to escape its memory by moving to New York, then to Paris. From reading *Black Power* it becomes clear that he hoped to find an Africa untainted by prejudice; a land, as he wrote, where humanity lived according to the laws of nature.

The Gold Coast was not the idyll he'd imagined, and perhaps on returning to Paris he abandoned any hope of paradise. As his fortunes faltered did he come to believe that racism had ensnared him with the finality it did his Uncle Hoskins in Arkansas?

Unallied to violence, racism can't kill directly. But it leads to a spiritual exhaustion. This seems to me a more likely reason for Wright's untimely death than murder.

Stripped of hope after returning from Ghana, did his heart give out having endured all it could bear?

Wright's passing led me to question the source of my dreams. At the time I took them as a sign of some ineffable unhappiness. Thinking back in the restaurant, though, I remembered the embarrassment of school in Queensbury after returning from Ghana. I'd say nothing when a kid called out 'jungle bunny' or Kevin Dyer shoved his face into mine and hissed 'black cunt'. The whole world seemed to be against me then. So maybe it was no surprise that I dreamed about shadowed snipers years later.

And perhaps this was why, when I finally saw the sniper, he turned out to have the same face as mine. He and I were the same person.

The shame of childhood was so severe I wanted to erase its memory. In my dreams I became the sniper, an emotionless killer determined to eradicate everything I secretly loathed about myself – my vulnerability, my pain, my childhood. I wanted to kill the past because it hurt too much.

That dream marked a climax – afterwards the nightmares faded away. Yet they seem more significant than ever now.

While I was in their grip, the boundaries between my internal reality and the outside world began to slip. My daytime fantasies of omnipotence – of machine-gunning passers-by on Upper Street – were fuelled by my terrors at night. This diagnosis would have struck me as melodram-atic at the time, but albeit in a minor way I believe I was showing signs of psychosis.

I asked for the bill and stood up.

However brief my brush with mental illness my experience was far from unique. In Britain, black people are six times more likely than whites to be diagnosed as schizophrenic. There is no biological explanation for the difference – only, it seems to me, the experience of racism we share growing up in the west.

I left my table and opened the door on to the street.

The insistence with which prejudice insinuates itself into everyday life is enough to leave you doubting your own faculties. You wonder if you've made up the sly expression of a work colleague or the patronizing tone of the bank clerk. Or you succumb to paranoia as Wright did because the difference between fantasy – a government plot to ruin your career – and reality – the State Department tapping your phone – is no longer discernible.

The search for a place beyond discrimination led Wright to Ghana. I formed the same goal the morning I woke up and found I'd shot myself dead in a dream. Until then the idea of returning to Ghana had barely appealed. What would I find there apart from faded memories, I asked myself?

In its wake I began to wonder what the effects of spending the rest of my life in Britain would be. Supposing the dreams returned with greater force? Would I end up acting on them? I prevaricated for years before buying a ticket. I was afraid that once I got there nothing would change. But my decision was forged that night.

I stepped out of the restaurant on to the same streets as Wright fifty years earlier. Were the words that came to me now the same as those in his head then? This is what I thought: you can't escape the past. It stays with you however far you run.

IV

I left Kumasi the next day. I was heading north to Bolgatanga, the last major town before the Ghanaian border with Burkina Faso. In a few more days I'd have crossed the country. My journey would be over.

When I arrived at the bus station I discovered that I could make a detour to Bolgatanga via Mole National Park. It was about 200 miles off my route, but there was a bus leaving from Kumasi that evening. It would arrive at the park the following morning. I could spend a couple of days watching elephants, baboons and gazelles, then take another bus to the border.

My entire relationship with wild animals had been conducted through Regent's Park Zoo and Hollywood movies. I told myself the detour would salve the affront of *Zulu*, *Congo*, *King Solomon's Mines* or any of the other films in which white adventurers hacked through the jungle while natives lobbed spears at them from the bush. The real reason was that I just like elephants. I like their scale, their density, the oblique delicacy of their trunks, and I wanted to see some close up without bars in the way. So I bought a ticket to Mole. The bus left in two hours. I sat on a wooden bench in the station and watched a scrum of passengers do battle with the laws of physics as they tried to shove their bags and boxes into the hold.

The sun set. Departure time approached. Outside the station I heard the sound of bleating. A group of men walked into the loading bay followed by a flock of goats. The goats milled around the bus. They scattered the concrete with droppings. The scent of urine filled the station. Herding them together, the men hauled and pushed the animals on to the roof of the bus one after the other until they were all roped by the ankles. After prolonged exertion the goats were all fastened down and the men stood looking up at their handiwork, glistening with effort, as the goats chorused their discontent from the roof.

I climbed on board feeling agitated and miserable at the drama I'd just witnessed. My low mood wasn't improved in any way by the slogan of the bus company, which was written on the seat in front of me. It said, 'We'll Get You There Alive.'

For a moment I thought of fleeing the station, and the country, altogether, just as Wright had when the omens mounted so intolerably against him. Up on the roof the goats started to scream. Blithely the driver turned up the volume on his radio and steered the bus out of the station into the night. It was too late for anything but to keep going.

I didn't know what to expect when I finally arrived at Bolgatanga. The north was an unknown proposition to me. Until 1907 it had been a separate state from the rest of the Gold Coast. Even now it remained culturally and physically divided from the south. In comparison to the zealous Christianity of Kumasi, many of its people were Muslims, their land given over to vast dry plains punctuated by millet fields and baobab trees. I drifted to sleep as the bus left the city, only to be woken by a wailing that sounded like a crying baby. It was coming from outside the bus.

I peered into the blackness. I couldn't see anything. Then a white shape flashed by the window. The bus jerked to a stop. The blur materialized into the form of a goat, screaming horribly. It had slipped from the roof and come swinging past the window by the rope tied to its leg.

The driver got out. He stood scratching his head. Some of the other men from the bus came to stand beside him. The animal carried on yelling. A chorus of screams answered it from the roof. A lively discussion broke out among the men about how to refasten it. None of them seemed eager to tackle its thrashing legs or the screaming of its comrades on the roof. From the back of the bus an old man in a djellaba hobbled forward, his face as worn as bark and his hands tough as hide. He looked like someone who'd wrangled with a few recalcitrant animals in his time. Hitching up his djellaba, he clambered on to the roof amid the flock's furious bleating. I heard his footsteps above me and the sound of his voice, loud then gradually softening as he hauled the dangling goat back to the roof and calmed the flock down. The old man climbed back to the ground.

He took his place at the back of the bus without another word. The rest of the men returned to their seats in bashful silence. The driver started the bus back down the highway.

I fell asleep again. When I opened my eyes it was near midnight. We weren't moving. The bus was pulled over on the edge of a field. The door stood open. Most of the passengers were outside. Some were sitting on the grass talking. Others had stretched out asleep on mats. Across the aisle from me a woman wearing a headscarf and a tired expression was cradling her sleeping baby.

'What happened?' I asked.

She rolled her eyes to the ceiling.

'It's too much, oh. The bus, it break down.'

'Can't we fix it?'

'We have to stay here tonight. The relief bus doesn't come till morning. This is what we've come to in Ghana. Even the bus cannot take us from one place to another without trouble.'

She was staying on the bus with her baby, said the woman. If I wanted I could borrow her mat.

'This is all we can do in the country. Unless we help each other the devil might as well take us all now.'

I climbed down into the warm night and unrolled the mat near a group of men clustered round a radio. I lay on my back listening to the murmur of their conversation for a long time. Trucks rumbled along the highway, their headlights flaring our camp into temporary radiance. For all the inconvenience of the emergency stop, it was more pleasant sleeping outside than in the stuffiness of the bus.

Even the goats were slumbering peacefully. I was exhausted, and as I lay on my back it seemed to me that I was falling upward into the sky, into the embrace of a darkness without limits.

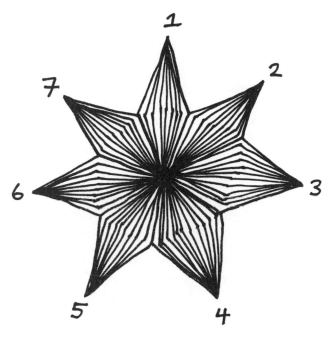

The elephants of Mole – Chris Ofili's vision of freedom –
Flying ace Alhaji – Bob Marley day in Bolgatanga –
Tupac and Osama – Hegel and racial science – The
border of Ghana – Inside the slave camp – W. E. B.
DuBois and The Souls of Black Folk – Kodwo and
Black Atlantic Futurism – Sun Ra and the rings of Saturn
– The City of London – Caribs' Leap

I

From a distance they hardly looked real. I worked the lenses of my binoculars until they sprang closer and I could make out the delicacy with which they wound their trunks through the branches and plucked at the leaves higher up the tree. As abruptly as they'd emerged a few minutes before, they retreated into the bush and I was left gazing at a deserted waterhole.

I'd arrived at Mole the previous evening and checked into the park hotel, which stood on a hilltop overlooking the 5,000-square-kilometre natural reserve. At the bottom of the hill lay the waterhole where I'd found the elephants gathered when I woke in the morning. A trekking group was leaving from the hotel in a few minutes to explore the area surrounding it. I hurried to join them and arrived as Solomon, the guide, was just finishing his introductory speech.

'We must be silent, silent, when we get close to the elephants,' he said. 'If one of them flares its ears get behind me. It's about to attack.'

He slapped the wooden butt of his rifle for emphasis and led the way down the hill into the bush, spiky leaves scratching at hands and a mosquito making experimental sorties around my head. We'd been trekking for an hour when he raised his hand. The waterhole was directly ahead. Six elephants stood at its far edge. One of the larger ones spread out its ears and waded into the pool. The others followed, dissolving themselves into the muddy water. Solomon pointed to a cloud of white tickbirds approaching above the trees.

'That means there are more elephants coming,' he whispered. 'The elephants move quiet, quiet, but the birds can tell you where they are.'

The trees across the lake seemed to part by their own volition. A dozen elephants materialized at the waterside. Breaking free of their parents, two calves plunged into the lake, their trunks peeking above the surface like periscopes. The rest of the herd followed them into the water. Even close up I had the sensation of watching mythical beasts, like coming across a herd of grazing unicorns.

By the time Solomon led us back to the hotel I started to notice there were creatures all around us. Green monkeys rustled through the trees. I spotted a golden antelope dash across a clearing. Arranged in perfect descending order of size and seniority, a family of warthogs crossed the path in front of us, their tails waving briskly like antennae.

I returned to my room, but by noon the heat was suffocating. I pulled on a hat and followed a trail leading to the small village near the hotel. The path led past a rubbish dump of watermelon rinds, mango stones and other discarded food. As I approached a troop of baboons was rooting through the garbage. I held still, expecting them to bolt at my presence, but they were too busy foraging to look up. While I was walking past one of the big males, shoulders trimmed with fur, cuffed an adolescent on the nose, triggering a chorus of shrieks among the troop audible all the way to the village.

The village itself looked deserted. The sun, I decided, must have driven everyone inside. Across from the main square, though, I made out Solomon crouched beside the wall of the school. A group of adults and children had gathered behind him. Solomon's rifle was drawn and, as I approached, he put his finger to his lips.

'Be careful. Stay behind me. It's Action.'

'What kind of action?'

'No. Action.'

'Action?'

'Look.'

I pushed my head round the corner. An elephant stood in the middle of the schoolyard chewing leaves off a tree.

'That's Action,' said Solomon. 'He's a young male. It's always trouble when he comes. Last month he stepped on someone's bicycle and crushed it. Today, this. Always trouble.'

I peered back round the wall. Action was staring at us. I could see his dark brown eyes and the curl of his lashes. The elephant flared his ears. Solomon curled his finger round the trigger of his rifle. I felt the sweat trickle down the inside of my shirt. Action regarded us in silence. He cocked back his head, yawned, then ambled out of the yard.

Solomon lowered his rifle. The children ran out from behind the wall and started waving their arms around like trunks.

'How often does an elephant come into town?' I asked.

Solomon took off his hat and wiped his forehead.

'All the time. Only Action's a problem, though. The others never come very near.'

We walked past the rubbish tip. The baboons had retired and a pair of warthogs was truffling at the remains.

'It seems as if there are just as many animals in the village as we saw down at the waterhole this morning,' I said.

'They know they'll find food here. They've got used to the people. Why go foraging in the bush when you can just come here?'

'So we didn't even need to go trekking? We could have just stayed here and let them come to us?'

Solomon shrugged.

'The tourists expect to see animals in their natural habitat. So we take them on tours. But this village is part of the park. Just because they're feeding on rubbish doesn't mean they're not behaving naturally. The tourists don't like to think of this as nature. It's only if you come into the village that you see it's all part of the same thing.'

Solomon left me at the edge of the village. I returned to the hotel turning over our conversation in my head. Every time I thought I had Ghana figured out I discovered another contradiction. Now it turned out even the wildlife park wasn't that wild.

That evening I ate dinner alone on the terrace of the hotel restaurant. Out of the dark giant scarab beetles hove towards the candle on my table and crashed on to the white tablecloth. They lay on their backs, legs kicking ineffectually, until I turned them over and helped them whirr away.

It seemed to me I had as much relationship to the reality of Ghana as the beetles did to the flame. Its outline flickered before me. But every time I stretched out to touch it I found myself on the floor with my legs waving in the air.

As I ate I recalled visiting the artist Chris Ofili at his house near Brick Lane. We'd spent the afternoon talking and drinking tea. The scent of cardamom percolated his living room from one of the many Bangladeshi restaurants nearby, and our conversation was periodically interrupted by the cassette tape of a chanting imam, borne through the open door of a Muslim grocery shop.

Ofili told me he was born in Manchester. Although his parents were Nigerian, he had been to Africa only once. That occasion was a student visit to Zimbabwe in 1992. Taken on a trip to a safari park, Ofili became captivated by the balls of elephant dung which lay half-hidden in the long grass, emerald-coloured beetles swarming over their surface so that they glittered like jewels.

Returning to Britain he made a visit to London Zoo and left with a bucket of dung. He fixed it to his paintings, decided he liked the effect and continued to use it on all his canvases. At the time Ofili was painting with a palette of brilliant colours – ceruleans, limes, fuchsias, sunset oranges – which he coated beneath thick layers of glaze.

Across the surface of the paintings he scattered the cut-out heads of African-American movie stars and rappers such as the Wu-Tang Clan, Dr Dre and the Notorious B.I.G. In 'The Holy Virgin Mary', his depiction of the black Madonna came adorned with breasts, buttocks and vaginas clipped from porn magazines with titles such as *Black Tail* and *Black Magic*.

The works drew scandal, but Ofili maintained his aim was to create a transformative universe in which all of the calumny heaped upon black people as sexualized, outlaw figures became the primal matter for a new order of beauty, just as elephant dung, seen through grass, might resemble emeralds. When he was eleven, Ofili told me, his parents split up and his father returned to Lagos. Ofili had not seen him since or ever travelled to Nigeria. Nevertheless, in 2002 he staged an exhibition of paintings inspired by his impressions of Africa. They showed an arcadia of palm trees, blissful lovers and red, black and green sunsets.

'I find it interesting that I've not been there,' he said that afternoon. 'How can I make the paintings I have without doing so? It's a contradiction. But you can ignore reality. Forget there's disease and conflict there. Forget it's a bit too hot and you can't understand the languages. Forget about all those things. It can still be the beautiful land of promise if you choose to imagine it that way.'

Recalling our conversation in Mole it seemed to me there was a divide between the idea and the reality of Africa. I'd spent my time in Ghana trying to resolve the distinction. By contrast Ofili painted Africa from imagination. The result was still an evocation of the truth as he saw it.

Maybe I'd been looking too hard for the answer when it already lay in front of me. In the darkness beyond the candle on my table there were parallel worlds in which black lovers kissed beneath red, black and green skies. Beyond those lay yet further galaxies of black freedom and beauty. Infinite versions of Africa unfolded through the night. Instead of trying to resolve all the paradoxes I came across, what if I accepted that Ghana was made up of multiple histories? If the country was born out of contradiction, maybe there was room enough to find my own vision of Africa?

It came to me that the best way to make sense of my journey would be to get to the end of it. Mole was less than a day from the border. I decided to leave as soon as possible for Bolgatanga. I looked at my watch. Midnight. No way out. But the idea had seized hold of me. Looking back I see now that I imagined the border as a place of release. I could stop feeling guilty about Joseph de Graft. I could surrender the memory of the coup and my bedroom fights with Kodwo. With hindsight I can see that was asking a lot from a simple inland border post. At the time I couldn't wait to leave.

II

'You can't leave,' said Solomon.

'Why?'

'It's impossible.'

'This is ridiculous.' I unfolded a tourist map and traced my finger along the road that snaked from Mole to Bolgatanga through 200 miles of bush. 'There's a bus that runs all the way from here. What's the problem?'

'Today's Sunday. It's not running. You'll have to wait until tomorrow.'

'Monday's no good,' I heard myself whine. 'It's got to be today.'

'What's the hurry?' said Solomon. 'Come with me today. I'll take you into the bush. We'll go looking for leopard.'

'It's no use. I have to go today. I can't explain.'

Solomon contemplated the mud on his boots.

'The only way to do it would be by taxi. But that's madness.'

'A taxi? That's brilliant.'

'Are you crazy? It will cost a fortune.'

'No, no, it's genius.'

I felt suddenly reckless. I was a needle tipping into the red zone. Lights flashed in my head. Clarions blared.

'I don't care about the money. Let's sort it out.'

I'd woken up that morning seized by the same urge to reach the border as the previous night. It seemed to me that only by arriving at the end of my journey could I stop to figure out what the trip had meant to me. However ordinary the border post itself might be, the prospect of reaching the end of the road was something I couldn't get out of my mind.

'I need to go, Solomon. Will you help me?'

We stood in silence, my question hovering between us, then without replying he disappeared down a cinder track to the village. An hour later Solomon returned, looking grave.

'None of the drivers wants to take you. They said the roads are too bad. They're right, you should wait till tomorrow. But anyway I carried on asking and . . .'

His words were drowned out by the whine of an engine as a tiny Korean Kia hatchback ground its way up the cinder path. Its orange-and-white livery shone with wax. Its hubcaps gleamed. A cloud of dust billowing behind it, the car pulled up at our feet.

'That's Alhaji,' said Solomon, pointing to the grinning youth behind the wheel. 'He was all I could get.'

Alhaji stuck his thumb up like a Spitfire pilot in his cockpit. I thought I saw Solomon shudder slightly.

'He doesn't speak much English. You know you can still just take the bus tomorrow. It would be better than going with this boy.'

'Thanks, Solomon, but I have to leave.'

He shook my hand, and I jumped into the passenger seat. Alhaji gunned the engine. An Arabic pop song wailed from the stereo. We skidded away down the cinder track. Solomon shrank from sight in the side-view mirror. Even after he'd disappeared I could still see the disconsolate expression on his face. In a distant place within myself I realized the taxi fare was more than his monthly wage. It was too late for regrets, though. I had a border to reach.

Humming to his cassettes, Alhaji hunkered down behind the wheel pushing his car hard. Bushes and low trees flickered past the open windows.

'I have friend in Bolga,' said Alhaji. 'She is good friend, you know.' He laughed through yellow teeth. I guessed the car hadn't been polished for my benefit.

We'd been travelling for two hours when he turned the Kia off the tarmac road and took us down a dirt track scattered with stones and boulders.

'Is this a shortcut?' I shouted above the engine.

A boulder loomed. Shoulder muscles bunching beneath his shirt, Alhaji swung us around it. He shot me a quick look.

'This is road. To Bolga. Yes.'

'Is it like this all the way to Bolgatanga?' I asked.

Alhaji did the thumbs-up again. In different circumstances – at dawn, say, with the silvery glow of the English Channel coming into view below at the end of a successful mission – it might have been reassuring. As it was I reached for the roof strap and held on as tightly as possible.

'Slower. We go slow.'

'Slow?' said Alhaji.

'Yes, slow.'

'OK. No problem.'

My head snapped back against the seat as the Kia accelerated along the dirt trail.

'No, slow,' I said.

'Yes, no slow,' cackled Alhaji, hunching low behind the wheel.

We burned along the track. Dust plumed behind us like the contrails of a jet engine. By my reckoning we'd already covered a third of the distance – I was starting to admire Alhaji's skill. We were leading the field in the inaugural Mole–Bolgatanga rally. The going was tough, but Team Eshun had been breaking records all morning. If we didn't get reckless we'd make it to Bolga by mid afternoon.

It was at that moment the Kia hit a hump in the road and launched itself into space. For a second we hung above the ground, the front wheels of the car spinning noiselessly and neither of us daring to breathe. Then we plunged back to earth with an ominous crunch. The car shuddered to a halt. We clambered out into a cloud of ochre dust. Its right front side had caved in on impact. Alhaji swung himself underneath the carriage.

'Is axle broken. Car smash.'

He sat up and wiped the dust from his face. I felt a wave of anger at the sight of him.

Thanks to flying ace Alhaji we were stranded in the middle of nowhere. If he hadn't been in such a hurry to see his girlfriend we'd have made it to Bolgatanga easily. Why couldn't he have slowed down when I told him to? I kicked a stone and watched it bounce among the dried-out bushes by the roadside and settle into the dust.

'We can't stay out here for long,' I said. 'The heat'll kill us if we don't get moving.'

Alhaji took the front, while I put my shoulder to the boot. We started pushing the Kia along the track. Its wheels sprayed us with dust. The sun beat on our heads. Dust bit into my eyes. I ducked my head and carried on shoving. Each step forward seemed to take hours. But the next time I looked up we were surrounded. A gang of boys had materialized out of the bush and were gathered round the car, chattering with Alhaji.

'They say village ahead,' he called from their midst. Jostling for handholds, the boys started to run the car along the track. Unable to keep up with their pace, I stood in the road catching my breath as they disappeared over an incline. The afternoon fell abruptly still.

None of this was Alhaji's fault, I told myself, following the car tracks. What difference would it have made if I'd left for Bolgatanga tomorrow? Why was it so important to reach the border immediately anyway?

Before I found an explanation I arrived at a clearing set back from the road. The boys had pushed the car to its edge and were still swarming round it as Alhaji examined the damage.

A group of men sat beneath a tree drinking from a calabash which they passed between them. They waved me over. An old man stood up as I approached. He wore a purple tracksuit and a toothless grin.

'Car no good,' he said.

I was forced to agree.

'Do you have mechanic?' I asked.

The question seemed to amuse him. I got a good view of his gums. He said his name was Hassan and he had his own moped. For a small fee, he was prepared to ride to the next town and look for a mechanic. I gave him 10,000 cedis and watched him putter away from the clearing on his ancient motorcycle.

Help might be some time arriving, I concluded.

Team Eshun makes unscheduled stop on the Mole–Bolgatanga rally. Duration: unknown.

I returned to the car. Alhaji was slumped by its side. He looked as forlorn as the vehicle itself.

'Mechanic?' he said.

'No mechanic,' I said. 'He come soon.'

An impression of Hassan carousing in the bars of the next town came to mind, but I dismissed it right away. There was a limit to how much fun an old man could have on 10,000 cedis – even one with a purple tracksuit and his own moped.

Alhaji would be here for a while. And because of me he'd wrecked the car that was his livelihood. I counted off 500,000 cedis and handed them to him. It was his fare for the whole trip to Bolgatanga. Now it might just cover the cost of repairs. Before he left Hassan had told me that if I waited by the roadside I'd be able to hitch a lift by truck the rest of the way to Bolgatanga.

I gave Alhaji a parting thumbs-up. He didn't look

up. I felt the last of my hunger to reach the border evaporate. I remembered Solomon's expression when I'd left Mole that morning. Through his eyes I must have looked like some pith-helmeted explorer riding into the jungle on a palanquin. He hadn't been sad to see me go. He was disgusted. Just as much as I'd been trying to figure out Ghana's contradictions, I had to accept my own. I'd spent almost all my life in a white country. How could I not have imbibed some of its prejudices along the way?

Europe looked down on Africa. Maybe I'd been doing the same thing? How else to explain shouting at bank managers and sneering at preachers while checking into a beach hotel with its own security guards? Does living in a white country make you, in some way, white, I asked myself, as I said goodbye to Alhaji.

An answer came to me while standing by the track waiting for a ride. We are not creations of our environment so much as its interpreters. In the three decades since I was a child, Britain had changed from a place where kids carved National Front logos into their desks at school, to somewhere more open and less fearful of change. Each person of colour living there had helped to create that shift. By doing nothing more nor less than being ourselves each of us had altered the nature of Britain. We'd made it over in our own image.

In the same way, it was impossible to arrive in Ghana without bearing some traits of the west. Nevertheless, the way I behaved was my responsibility, not the result of culture or genetics, and that was surely a cause for optimism.

Maybe you can't undo the past, but the present is mutable. All I could do as I travelled was accept that at different times I'd be naive, excited, angry or behave like an idiot. None of those elements defined who I was any more than a self-important bank manager or Joseph de Graft represented the whole of Ghana.

There was no template to being African or English. You just had to make it up as you went along.

III

As penance for my foolishness, I checked into a room at the Catholic Mission centre once I reached Bolgatanga. The room smelled of mould and the bedsheets were marked with ominous stains. In the morning I was woken by the sound of pigs rooting through a rubbish heap outside my window. Above the communal washroom at the end of the passage, a notice read: 'Please do not urinate in the bathroom.' I spent the whole of my shower on tiptoe. Just as I reached the breakfast table a bishop in his purple robes heaped the last of the scrambled eggs on to his plate with a contented smile.

I gave up on breakfast and crossed the road to order coffee in the whitewashed courtyard of the much grander Black Star Hotel. The waiter took my order and vanished into the interior of the bar. From its depths I heard a radio playing 'No Woman, No Cry', followed by 'Redemption Song', then 'Natural Mystic'.

'Why all the Bob Marley?' I asked as he returned with my drink.

'You don't know? It's Bob Marley day. All over Ghana we celebrate his birthday today.'

'I didn't realize he was so popular here.'

'But of course. In the whole of Africa he is for the black man. His songs are for freedom.'

'Aren't you already free?'

'Yes, but I'm poor. Without money you don't have freedom. That's why we love Bob Marley so much in Africa. He speaks for people like us.'

The waiter returned to the bar. 'Buffalo Soldier' drifted into the courtyard. I drank my coffee. It struck me that the freedom he heard wasn't so much to do with the absence of oppression as the embrace of possibility. Bob Marley sang for the waiters and market women and Small Boys who dreamed of achieving more than they were born to in Africa. If it was Bob Marley day in Bolgatanga they were probably celebrating his birth in Nairobi, Kinshasa and Bamako, too.

I experienced a renewed surge of shame at my taxi ride – as if I'd allied myself with all the forces holding back the ordinary people of Africa by taking that trip. Leaving the hotel I drifted down the street past a row of open-air workshops where craftsmen sat chiselling figurines of tribal warriors out of wood. In the shade beneath a tree a portrait painter had propped his pictures of prominent Ghanaians such as Kwame Nkrumah and Kofi Annan. One of the paintings caught my eye. It was split into thirds, a triptych, with a different subject in each section – Bob Marley, Tupac Shakur and Osama Bin Laden. All three rendered as nobly as the neighbouring statesmen. Just looking at the picture made my head reel. I shut my eyes against the glare of multiple worlds colliding.

By coming to Ghana I'd hoped to find something of myself that was lost. How was I different from Capitein or Richard Wright or any of the other travellers who arrived seeking certainties only to discover more questions? Instead of a singular place I'd discovered a country making and remaking itself under the gaze of its elective gods. Bob Marley was the icon of contemporary Africa. In another way Osama played the same role. I remembered seeing T-shirts of him for sale on the roadside soon after I'd arrived in Accra. I was surprised, but had given it little thought until I flicked through a copy of the magazine *Africa Today* at a newsstand in Kumasi. On a page of readers' photos I'd found a picture of a Ghanaian student on his way to a fancy-dress party wearing Osama's white beard and combat fatigues. There were those in Ghana who'd never measured the moral weight of September 11th. In their minds Osama was simply a symbol of Third World resistance to the west.

His words or politics didn't interest them – only his image. It was no different than westerners wearing Che Guevara T-shirts while remaining ignorant of the principles of revolutionary socialism.

But what about Tupac? A conversation floated into my mind from my cousin Kobby's visit to London five years earlier. We'd been walking along Tottenham Court Road when a BMW drove past blasting Tupac's 'Keep Ya Head Up'.

'You know he's not dead,' said Kobby.

'Who?'

'Tupac. He's still alive.'

'Of course he's not. He was shot in Las Vegas last year.'

Kobby pushed up his chin as if he was trying to balance the weight of his superior knowledge upon it.

'They never found his body. Didn't you know? He's still out there.'

I started to tell him that Tupac had been cremated, his ashes had been scattered on his mother's farm in North Carolina, but I stopped myself, figuring that seventeen-year-olds needed their heroes. Instead I made him a cassette of Tupac's most recent album *Me against the World* and gave it to him as he was returning to Ghana.

'I played that tape all through school,' he told me in Accra.

We were driving through town. As we paused at the traffic lights, he leaned over and tugged something free from the mess in the glove compartment.

'Look, I played it until it broke,' he said, rattling the same cassette I'd given him five years before.

Why did Kobby love Tupac so much? Listening to him, I got the impression that Tupac said all the things that my cousin and his friends found difficult. Thug poet, street

intellectual, romantic gangsta, he was idolized by a generation of young Ghanaians. In his brusque lyricism, they saw
their own yearnings. They believed in Tupac as much as
their parents had believed in Nkrumah. It mattered no
more that he was American than it did that Bob Marley
was Jamaican-Scottish or Osama a Saudi. In Ghana all
three became African: the idols to a portrait painter in
Bolgatanga, a student in fancy dress and Kobby Mensah at
the wheel of his Golf.

What we see of our heroes is only what we choose to
observe, it struck me while looking at the painting. They
are figures of myth rather than reality. But then, of course,
myths can be real, too. In the hundreds of years since
building the first settlement at Elmina, Europe has been
spinning its tales of African inferiority. Writing in 1758,
the Swedish botanist Carl Linnaeus divided humanity
into three subspecies, describing *Homo africanus*, the least
developed, as: 'crafty, slothful, careless', with 'silken skin,
apelike nose and swollen lips'.

His words were later echoed by the plantation owner
Edward Long, whose bestselling book *The History of
Jamaica* extended Linnaeus's argument to suggest that
Africans were a separate species of humanity altogether
– one closer in kind to apes than Europeans. 'Ludicrous
as it may seem,' he concluded, 'I do not think that an
orang-outang husband would be any dishonour to an
Hottentot female.'

During the nineteenth century, the notion of the biological inferiority of Africans gathered pace. It was supported by philosophers such as Kant, Herder and Hegel, who noted in 1824 that: 'the Negro is an example of animal man in all his savagery and lawlessness.' His nature could be understood by a European 'no more than . . . that of a dog'. Fuelled by such sentiments the discovery of objective proof of Europe's racial superiority became one of the great scientific obsessions of the nineteenth century.

Whole new schools of thought rose up in its pursuit, from osteometry, craniology, craniometry and pelvimetry to phrenology, physiology, physiognomy and philology. In 1850, the Scottish anatomist Robert Knox wrote: 'Race is everything: literature, science, art – in a word, civilization depends on it.'

From the nineteenth into the twentieth century, the science of race became grimmer in theory and more furious in application. Racial thinking gave way to racial policy: eugenics programmes, forced sterilizations, yellow stars, train tracks into the Polish woods.

And all of it for nothing. Because race itself is no more than myth. Beneath skin colour there is no intrinsic difference between the peoples of Africa or Asia or Europe. Far from being everything, 'race' is nothing. It is a fiction. A lie contradicted by a drop of blood beneath the lens of a microscope. Yet its shadow does not fade.

So as I stood by the kerb in Bolgatanga, the veneration of Marley and Tupac and even Osama came to make sense to me. If race is indelible and, with it, the accumulated weight of western prejudice, what else is there to do but create our own heroes, and with them build new myths of freedom and resistance?

III

Squirming for comfort I peered out of the windscreen at the parched fields stretching away from the highway. The pregnant woman snapped off another bite of her chalk. She shifted position, nudging me closer to the edge of the seat. I clung to the dashboard and tried to lose myself again in the blank view outside. I'd imagined the final leg of my journey in more glorious terms.

At the artisans' row in Bolgatanga I'd hailed a taxi for the twenty-mile trip to the border. En route, the driver had picked up four passengers for the back and, just as I'd been congratulating myself on capturing the front seat, had stopped to pick up a heavily pregnant woman, who'd spent the journey so far nibbling on a stick of chalk. I'd been teetering between her and the gear stick since leaving Bolgatanga thirty minutes ago.

Without warning the driver pulled over to the edge of the highway. Before I could get my bearings the taxi was already bobbing as the pregnant woman pulled herself out. By the time I'd followed her the other passengers had vanished across the fields. Reversing his car the taxi driver skidded back up the road. Through the dust stirred by his tyres I saw a checkpoint ahead. I'd reached the border.

In the absence of a river or a mountain range, there can

often be an arbitrariness to inland frontiers. This is probably especially true in Africa, where the logic of colonial geographers becomes increasingly obscure with time. It was certainly the case with the Ghana–Burkina Faso customs post. Above the road ran a wooden arch with an uneven hand-painted sign that read 'Bye Bye Safe Journey'. Below it, customs officers in blue uniforms checked the passports of truck drivers crossing the twenty metres to Burkina Faso where staff in green uniforms waited to examine the same documents. Beyond them the parched fields gave way to crouching green mountains swathed at their summit in cloud.

A truck rumbled past coating me with dust. Millet seeds whorled in the air. Now that I'd reached it I saw that the frontier had nothing to offer me.

Maybe I should have known all along. Unlike, say, the white cliffs of Dover, there was nothing symbolic about the border's presence. It was a purely functional entity that existed on maps and in the minds of bureaucrats. I was furious with myself. The whole of yesterday's frenzied race had been for nothing. When I was in Mole the idea of reaching the border had seemed like a way to resolve the anxieties I'd accumulated during my trip. I didn't want to go back to London like Richard Wright, weighted down with sorrow. I'd told myself that an answer lay at the border. Now that I'd arrived, I saw how ridiculous that idea had been. There was nothing here to ease the memory of the coup or of Kevin Dyer's face. I'd crossed the whole of Ghana and I still couldn't say where I was from.

Now there was nowhere left to go. Tears sparked by roadside grit and disappointment blurred my sight.

I wiped my eyes and started to walk away from the customs post. Riding by in the taxi I'd noticed a small town a couple of miles back along the highway. I headed towards it feeling as dried out and flat as the surrounding fields.

The town turned out to be a scattering of houses with domed roofs and dark windows hidden behind high walls. None of them showed any sign of life apart from the last one. Outside it hung a sign reading 'Salman: Antiques for sale. Bicycles for hire'. I banged on the metal gates. At least I could go cycling for a couple of hours before I returned to the grubby Catholic Mission.

No answer. I banged again. I'd already begun walking away when a man's voice called after me.

He had a light-skinned, Arab complexion and quick, precise gestures that reminded me of a sparrow. 'Come, come,' he said, leading me through the courtyard of his house into a circular, windowless room with a rough clay floor. He gestured for me to sit down.

'I am Salman,' he said with a little bow. 'You have come for antiques, yes?'

Without waiting for an answer Salman started rooting through the leather bags and wooden chests scattered round the edges of the room. From their depths came herds of rearing elephants, snarling lions and tribal warriors. Their uniformly worn nature led me to suspect they'd originated with the craftsmen in Bolgatanga, then been kicked about in the dust for a while until they acquired an appropriately aged veneer.

The day wasn't getting any better.

I tried waving them away, but a small army of warriors and wildlife had built up on the clay floor before he finally accepted that all I wanted was to rent a bike.

'OK, my friend, I'll take you on a tour through the fields. We will go to see the slave camps.'

'I thought all the forts were in the south.'

'Not forts,' said Salman. 'Camps. From stone. Come with me. I'll show you.'

We wheeled two heavy upright bicycles out of the courtyard and pedalled into the fields. Salman led the way without any apparent effort while I laboured behind him, struggling to keep my bike from sinking into the sandy trail.

The idea of slave camps so far from the coast seemed bizarre. Yet the slave routes that terminated in Cape Coast and Elmina had begun in the north. Perhaps some evidence of them still remained.

We cycled for an hour, past 300-year-old farmhouses made of clay bricks, and cotton trees the pods of which had split open along the trail, exposing the cloudy fibres inside. Past guinea fowl picking at the soil and the trunks of giant baobab trees. I was sweating freely by the time Salman stopped.

The plains had given way to low, flat boulders. Before I could join him he'd already thrown down his bike and was scrambling across them. When I caught up with him

I saw that the rocks stretched for miles, growing in size to enormous boulders that lay scattered in the distance like the scree of a mountain range. Salman stood on the lip of a clearing formed by the rocks into a natural bowl. He stretched out his arms.

'This is the slave camp.'

All I could see was more boulders.

'It's just rocks,' I said. 'Where's the camp?'

'All around you,' said Salman, spreading his arms wide. 'The Arab slave raiders used to ride down from Niger and Mali. They'd capture slaves from the villages around here and make camp in these stones.'

He pointed into the bowl.

'If you look they form a natural defence from attack. The slaves would be held down there, and there'd be guards would stand up here to stop them from escaping or to keep the villagers from rescuing them.'

He began climbing down into the bowl.

'Slaves would be kept here for up to six months. They'd start with maybe twenty and only leave when there were around 200. Then they'd march to Salaga or Kumasi to sell them.'

'How could you live out here for that long?'

I followed him down to the floor of the bowl. The rocks curved around us in a high wall, cutting off a view of the plains. In the sudden coolness even the equatorial sun felt remote.

'See how this boulder is worn flat on top?' said Salman. 'This is what the slaves used for grinding millet.'

He pointed to another rock with shallow indentations on its surface.

'That's what they used as plates. They put the ground meal in there, mixed it with water and scooped it out with their hands.'

I followed him round the bowl.

You could see where slaves had scratched out a rudimentary board on the surface of some of the stones to play a game with pebbles similar to draughts. Knock hard on the larger boulders and they rang deep and hollow. At night, the slaves would play them like drums as they sang in memory of their homes. One stone stood in full sight of the sun. Salman knelt down beside it.

'This groove that runs round the base here – it comes from a chain. This was a punishment stone. If a slave tried to escape he was shackled here and left to die in the sun.'

A shiver ran along my arms. Slavery meant the denial of individuality. It tried to strip humans of their will as effectively as it stole them from their homes. Like the dungeons of Elmina castle, this camp was a factory for the breaking of the soul. Yet the evidence of resistance was scratched into its rocks. Each time they sang the slaves asserted their freedom. Every time they shared food they held on to their humanity.

We climbed out of the bowl. Salman cycled back to his house. I stayed behind among the boulders. Evening beckoned. In the waning light the rocks glowed pink and became warm to the touch.

A few years ago, travelling round the Caribbean island of Grenada, I'd come across the story of the island's indigenous people, the Caribs. Faced with the threat of enslavement by French forces in 1651 they went to war. They lost. But instead of surrendering the last forty Caribs leaped to their deaths into the sea. This seemed to me a story of victory rather than doom. Instead of chains the Caribs chose to die free. In doing so they ensured their memory lived on beyond them. More than three hundred years after their deaths, the cliff face they jumped from was still known as Carib's Leap.

Looking round the rocks it came to me that journeys never truly end. Lives are remembered by rocks. The past is renewed in our genes. In that respect, you never truly leave home. It stays with you even in the worst of times. Like the slave camp here or Carib's Leap, the desire for intimacy among humans never goes away. Where was I from? Maybe the answer was here, among the rocks. The same would be true for any black person born in the west. Wherever we'd settled we carried with us the collective memory of slavery. Like the generations who'd passed through the camp I'd found here, we faced the denial of our humanity every day in the west. Our answer was the inalienable fact of our aliveness. We sang among the rocks. We chose a leap into freedom rather than a life in chains.

Night had fallen by the time I returned to my bike. As I cycled along the track, farmers were lighting fires to burn out the roots of old plants. Very faintly, the chorus of 'So

Much Trouble in the World' floated towards me from someone's Bob-Marley-day celebration. My legs churned the pedals. A plume of dust rose behind me and settled back into the earth. I'd reached the end of my journey. There was nowhere left to go but back to London.

IV

From Bolgatanga I caught a string of buses south to Accra and prepared to catch my return flight. On the morning of my last day I visited the former home of W. E. B. DuBois. The founding father of the civil rights movement in America, William Edward Burghardt DuBois was born in 1868 and launched the National Association for the Advancement of Coloured People in 1909. In 1961, having exiled himself from what he considered a reactionary and racist United States, he settled in Accra at the age of ninety-three.

His house, a gift from the Ghanaian government, stood in a discreetly affluent neighbourhood not far from the airport. Following his death in 1963, it was converted into a museum. Unfortunately this turned out to be a lifeless place, full of faded exhibits and gloomy corridors. On the morning I arrived to look round there were no other visitors.

I'd made my trip with a specific goal in mind, and it was only after I'd left the main display room and explored the rest of the house that I discovered what I was looking for.

Down the end of a corridor around the back of the building, I discovered DuBois's study. Shelves of NAACP papers and hardback volumes of his writing lined the room. I started searching along their spines to find the book I wanted.

When I located it I tugged at the doors of the glass cabinet encasing the shelves. They swung open. A basement odour seeped into the room. I pulled out the book. My fingers ran across its embossed lettering: *The Souls of Black Folk*. DuBois had signed it at the front. The blue ink of his signature had faded, but the date was still legible – 1903. It was a first edition.

I started to read.

'Herein lie buried many things which, if read with patience, may show the strange meaning of being black here in the dawning of the twentieth century,' wrote DuBois. I followed his words down the page, losing myself in their rhythm as if it was the first time I'd read them. It was only when I looked up near the end of the first chapter that I realized I wasn't alone any more.

'We normally ask visitors not to touch the books.'

A museum guide stood in the doorway. He was wearing a name badge and an expression of fierce reproach. I became powerfully aware of a clock's harsh ticking on the wall and the rasp of a fly as it circled the room. A bead of sweat ran down the gully of my back like a ball bearing. The guide pulled the book from my hands and returned it to the shelves. He locked the glass cabinet and stood in front of it with his arms crossed.

'Please, I must ask you to leave now,' he said.

As I left the room he came to stand in the doorway. I could sense him watching me all the way down the corridor. However embarrassing it was to be caught, I consoled myself with the idea that, at least for a short while, I'd freed DuBois's spirit from the gloom of the museum.

At the back of the house I emerged into a large, well-groomed garden at the far end of which stood an octagonal summerhouse. A light rain had started to fall, and sheltering beneath the summerhouse roof I watched the water whisper into the grass, raising a warm mist into the air.

I was eighteen when I first discovered *The Souls of Black Folk*. I'd just finished my A levels, and feeling grown-up and sophisticated I'd spent the summer watching Russian science-fiction movies at the Scala repertory cinema and going to talks about black art and film theory at the Institute of Contemporary Arts.

Browsing through the shelves at the ICA bookshop I came across a copy of DuBois's book. I picked it up, flicked through it and put it straight back on the shelves. The language was too rich for my taste. In the places where the 'yea's and 'lo's were especially dense, it read like a cast-off from the Old Testament. I bought a copy of Richard Wright's memoir *Black Boy* instead.

Yet *The Souls of Black Folk* kept returning to my thoughts. In the book's opening chapter, DuBois told a story from his childhood. It is a bright morning in his New England home town of Great Barrington. At the wooden school-house, the eight-year-old DuBois is playing a game with the other children that involves swapping visiting cards. DuBois hands one of his cards to a girl who has recently joined the class. She shakes her head and turns away, refusing it. DuBois stands in the schoolyard trying to understand why she has rejected him. Gradually understanding dawns. She is white, and he is the only black child at the school. For the first time in his life he has been judged by the colour of his skin.

Like the lowering of a vast veil, wrote DuBois, that moment in the schoolyard was his coming of age. In that instant he understood that the birthright of black people was a 'double consciousness': an awareness that they stood inside and outside the white world at the same time. To be black in America meant always being a stranger – even in your home town.

When I eventually bought a copy of his book I realized how prophetic DuBois had been. Mannered tone aside, *The Souls of Black Folk* could have been written at the end of the twentieth century instead of its dawn. With his description of double consciousness, DuBois became the first writer to articulate the sensibility of black people born into the white world. He was also the first to argue that, far from being a drawback, our dual gaze was a blessing. It meant that we regarded life with an acuity white people could never muster. We watched for the bigotry cloaked in humour and the hesitations in speech that betrayed hostility. We used double consciousness to survive, and ultimately thrive, in the white world.

DuBois's words had stayed with me ever since that summer. They'd made sense for me growing up in Britain. They'd even given me a way to deal with the disorientation of returning to Ghana. Now, watching the rain fall into the grass, the book made me think of a conversation I had seven years ago with Kodwo. That was when I realized my brother had grasped the full, DuBoisian strangeness of life in Britain when we were still children.

V

Kodwo works by night.

Hunched over the screen of his Apple computer he writes into the early hours of the morning about music, architecture, cinema or whatever else he's curious about at the time. As a consequence, the best time to visit him at home is after midnight, when he will definitely be at his desk surrounded by a pile of books. Seven years ago he was living in a basement flat in Kensington. I'd been visiting friends nearby. On the way home I knocked on his door. It was 1.15 a.m. He didn't seem surprised to see me, even though I hadn't told him I was coming.

A single lamp illuminated his living room, revealing rows of drum 'n' bass records and stacks of paperback books heaped on the carpet. It struck me that Kodwo had transplanted the tone of our old bedroom to a new location, and I felt a familiar mixture of admiration and resentment as I sat on the sofa.

He brought in some mugs of instant coffee and we talked about the Alice Coltrane record on his stereo. Like most times we met there was a wariness to our conversation. We could talk easily enough about music or books, but since leaving Kingsbury neither of us had mentioned the coup or the years we spent squabbling in its aftermath. The effort of not doing so lent a brittleness to our conversation. It was as if we were both afraid that even mentioning the past would return us physically to the confines of our old bedroom.

Kodwo was a freelance journalist and earlier that year, at twenty-nine, he'd signed a contract to write a book. This was not welcome news. I'd always imagined myself as an author. The fact Kodwo had got there first felt like further proof that I'd never escape his shadow. For months I'd kept my distance from him until curiosity got the better of me and I'd come banging on his door in the night-time.

'So what's the book about?' I said, when there didn't seem anything left to discuss about Alice Coltrane.

Kodwo blew some of the steam off his coffee mug.

'Music and science fiction. What else is there?'

The book was called *More Brilliant than the Sun*. It was an exploration of a concept he called 'Black Atlantic Futurism' – a modernist impulse uniting an otherwise disparate set of black musicians, from the cosmic jazz of Alice Coltrane and Sun Ra in America to Lee 'Scratch' Perry's dub reggae in Jamaica and the drum 'n' bass of British acts such as 4 Hero and A Guy Called Gerald.

'That sounds great,' I said without much enthusiasm. I wanted to be pleased for him, but suddenly I felt exhausted.

I remembered how Kodwo and I had played football together in the garden when we were kids. I could tell if he was angry or excited or sad from the force and accuracy with which he kicked the ball. I'd thought then that I'd always be able to make out the shape of his hopes or secret desires. Even as adults we'd still sometimes run into each other wearing identical clothes as if our thoughts had followed the same pattern that morning. I'd taken that connection for granted once. But the past had come between us to such an extent that I wasn't sure what we had in common any more. We could carry on talking about music for ever, but that wouldn't stop the silence continuing to grow between us.

'Kodwo,' I said.

'What?'

'I ... I ...' I couldn't find the words to say how I'd looked up to him as a kid; how tired I was of being jealous of him as an adult; how much I wanted us to be friends.

'Nothing.'

I sipped some lukewarm coffee.

The Alice Coltrane record ran to a stop. The stereo made a humming noise. From the kitchen I heard a tap dripping into the sink.

'It's two o'clock. I should be going.'

Kodwo was swirling the last of the coffee in his mug. He didn't seem to hear me. Or perhaps he had something on his mind, too.

I'm tempted to describe what happened at that moment as a return of our childhood telepathy. No doubt the truth is less grand, though. He would probably have said what he did irrespective of what I was thinking. Even so it was still a surprise to hear.

If I'd felt isolated and afraid through our bedroom years, so, it transpired, had Kodwo.

'This book I'm writing, it's about us – you, me and Esi,' he said. 'It's going to be dedicated to the New Mutants – you remember them; they were the junior X-Men. That was us. The New Mutants are the outcasts. They don't fit in because they're too thoughtful for their own good. They don't have the street smartness society expects from its black kids.

'When I was younger I always felt too vulnerable. So I looked to books and records for clues as to how to behave. All the things I was into back then – the Roger Dean record sleeves, the *Dune* trilogy – they weren't just an escape. They gave me the tools to make my way through the real world. I was looking for things that affirmed my sense of alienation.

'That's why I went around school in the Dr Who scarf. Dr Who was a time-travelling eccentric alien who came to earth and bamboozled everybody. He was cryptic. He knew a lot of stuff, but he wasn't going to give it to you straight.'

'But I thought you were the one who had everything figured out,' I said. 'You were Reed Richards.'

Kodwo shrugged.

'Maybe. But very early on I had a feeling that we weren't like other young black kids. We hardly knew any for a start. And I was quite frightened of West Indian kids. They seemed tougher and more confident. Like they came from another world. One of my most painful memories is going to a rugby match and them hating Kingsbury High kids for being white and middle-class. They chased us out of their school. I felt really humiliated by what these black kids might think of me – did they see me as an honorary white kid? That was bad enough. But I had an even worse feeling. They knew me for what I was and they didn't like that either. It felt like I was being singled out for being shy and awkward instead of macho.

'You, me and Esi, we were a minority in a minority. I tried to turn that into an elitism. I always felt everybody around me was stupid. That's partly arrogance, but it seemed legitimate given the world insisted young black men were thugs. I tried to be proud of being intelligent. I felt other people's amazement that we existed. It was like being at ninety degrees to the rest of England.'

'It seemed like there was a lot to run from.'

'The fact that that included each other pains me, although it seems inevitable now. It wasn't that we fell out. It was more like drifting apart. Little by little we pulled away from each other. We didn't have a vocabulary for all the things we were going through. For being teenage, staying up late, staying out, discovering girls, discovering the outside world. We shared a room and eventually that wasn't enough to hold us together.'

'Have you ever thought about going back to Ghana? Sometimes I wonder if we'd be more at home there.'

He rolled his eyes.

'That's not the point. I'm not interested in trying to reclaim some idea of the past. Africa's not this idyllic place. It's a mistake to assume that you can go back to some kind of motherland. That doesn't exist. The only thing is to create a place of your own where you feel at home.'

Kodwo examined the bottom of his mug. A car pulled away outside with a squeal of tyres. I looked at my brother's face in the lamplight. How much did I really know about him? I'd imagined I could see into his head but until now I'd never seen past its surface.

If I still believed in science fiction I would have said that we were one person living two separate existences, each of us carrying an indelible sadness through life in the mistaken belief that we were alone in the world. I wanted to get up and hug him so that, for a moment at least, we really could become one.

There was another way to reach him, however.

'Tell me more about the book,' I said.

Black Atlantic Futurism began in 1955, said Kodwo. That was the year Sun Ra announced he was born on Saturn.

Born in 1914 as Herman Poole Blount, Ra played piano

in the nightclubs and strip joints of Alabama, before declaring at the age of forty-one that, as Sun Ra, his true home was among the stars. Bald-headed and draped in golden robes, he described himself as the captain of an interstellar vessel on a mission of enlightenment. He had lifted off from Saturn and arrived in ancient Egypt, home of the most advanced scientific knowledge in the world at the time. From Egypt he'd travelled to the twentieth century, only to discover that the black origins of civilization had been erased by white people. Western history was a lie, said Ra. In its place, he would build his own mythology in which African science had continued to thrive and black people came to sail the cosmos.

'See, here's the thing,' said Kodwo. 'What if Sun Ra wasn't making it all up? Supposing everything he said was true? What's so strange about the idea of a black man from Saturn? It's not that odd, really. Not if you think that the entire history of black people in the west can be described as a case of abduction by aliens.'

Black people were kidnapped from Africa and transported across a vast distance inside a strange vessel. When they arrived in the New World, they were put to work under white overlords. Families were separated. Countrymen forbidden to speak their own language. Under law they were not even regarded as human beings.

'For all the difference it made they might as *well* have been taken to another planet. The whole thing is pure science fiction.'

★

Rain continued hissing into the museum lawn. Beneath the roof of the summerhouse I remembered that DuBois had written a science-fiction story in 1920 called 'The Comet'. I'd discovered it while reading through an anthology of black science fiction some years ago, and the plot returned to me in the garden by slow degrees, like a ship emerging from the fog.

In the story, the population of New York is wiped out by the poisonous gas trail of a comet. Oblivious to the disaster a black labourer works in the tunnels beneath the city. He surfaces to find the streets piled with corpses. The dead have fallen where they stood in their grey woollen suits and brown leather shoes. The labourer starts to walk through the city. For days he finds no sign of life. Then he discovers a young woman. She is the white daughter of a wealthy businessman. He has never addressed a white woman as his equal. The only black people she has ever known are maids and doormen. They stare at each other fearfully. Yet in the knowledge of their isolation the nature of their gaze changes. To survive, they have to see through the other's eyes. The hope of new life rests with them. They begin to recognize the humanity in the face staring back at them. And the beauty, too. They lean together with parted lips.

At that moment a group of survivors arrives from outside Manhattan, where they'd escaped the comet's path. They include the young woman's fiancé and the labourer's wife. Normality begins to reassert itself. But the kiss that never was suggests the possibility of a new order. A future based on love and respect between the races not hostility. A world that, in 1920, seemed no more real than science fiction.

Only in the 1960s, centuries after their ancestors were first taken to the New World, did black people in America gain the same legal freedoms as whites. The struggle for civil rights reached its apogee on Wednesday, 28 August 1963, when a crowd of 250,000 gathered around the length of the Reflecting Pool in Washington to hear Martin Luther King proclaim their right to liberty.

At midnight of the preceding day DuBois had passed away in his bed in Accra, aged ninety-five. On the afternoon of 28 August his body was laid out in a bronze open casket beneath the roof of the octagonal summerhouse. Family friends including Maya Angelou and Betty Shabazz, the wife of Malcolm X, mixed on the lawn with government dignitaries. Nkrumah arrived in a black Zilli limousine. He hugged the widow, Shirley Graham DuBois, and stood for a while over the coffin with his head bowed. A state linguist poured a libation consigning DuBois's soul to the heavens. At that point, a shower of rain fell upon the garden, forcing the mourners to dash for cover. To the Ghanaians present, it was a sign that the passage to the afterworld had opened to receive DuBois's spirit.

The casket was draped in the red, gold and green colours of the Ghanaian flag. It was placed on a military gun carriage and drawn along 28th February Road. At Independence Square, several thousand spectators gathered to watch it pass along the way to its final resting place at Christianborg Castle.

Flanked by an honour guard in ceremonial scarlet jackets, Nkrumah gave a speech describing DuBois as the greatest scholar ever produced by the Negro race. To the notes of the last post delivered by a bugler from the Central Army Band, the coffin was lowered into the ground beside the walls of the castle.

In Washington, Roy Wilkins, secretary of the NAACP, asked the crowd to lower their heads in memory of DuBois. Among the audience some wondered if his soul wasn't then passing over the masses at the Reflecting Pool. Perhaps, they said, it lent strength to Martin Luther King, who, at 3.40 that afternoon, began to speak of his dreams with a resonance that changed the course of the American republic.

What journey does the spirit make after it leaves the body?

As I left Ghana on board a British Airways plane that evening, I pictured the unfolding night of space. *More Brilliant than the Sun* was published in 1998. The cover shows a photograph of the rings of Saturn taken by the *Voyager II* space probe as it hurtles beyond the frontier of our solar system. Maybe this is how we can imagine the spirit's path: a solitary traveller exploring the stars, the only destination marked 'Further'.

VI

It was early morning when I arrived at Heathrow. Even after the plane screamed to a halt at Terminal 3 I had the impression that I was still in motion. The glass buildings across the tarmac looked out of focus. Inside the airport, a tannoy squawked alien announcements. Passengers jostled for their suitcases at the luggage carousel. My head spun. I smelled fried fish and jollof rice. I saw a plain of red earth.

A tube carried me into central London. At Euston, where I changed trains, a mouse scuttled along the platform, unnoticed by the commuters. I emerged at Moorgate station and fought through the tide of office workers heading for the City. As I approached my flat, which lies in a maze of streets behind Finsbury Square, office blocks gave way to disused print works and parking lots constructed from the craters of Luftwaffe bombing missions.

In their sudden emptiness, the streets made me think of the slave camp in Bolgatanga. What did it take to survive in a place like that? Maybe nothing more than ordinary will. The same spirit that enabled the descendants of slaves to build a future for themselves in the New World. In both cases the refusal to believe you were anything less than human.

Soon after the last of the nightmares that ran through my late twenties, I realized I needed a break from London. That was when I went to Grenada. I spent a week there swimming and reading novels and learning to sleep without having the blinds open to ward off the darkness.

Reading a tourist guide to Grenada I discovered the story of the Caribs. I found I couldn't get it out of my mind. Their fate moved me so deeply that I hired a car and drove to the far end of the island to find the cliff face from which they'd jumped. I stood at the edge of Caribs' Leap picturing how they must have been herded across their land by the French; how they'd gathered above the cliffs knowing that to return meant capture while only the waves lay ahead. And it struck me at that moment that nothing ever truly dies. Long after we pass away, we are remembered by molecules in the air that recycle our hair and skin. Even the echoes of the Big Bang are still being heard across the universe.

Thinking that way made the idea of returning to Ghana much easier to contemplate. I'd spent my adult life trying to run from my childhood. It had caught up with me in my dreams. The nightmares had stopped. But I was still afraid that going back would mean reliving the past in all its detail. I wanted to be free. Yet perhaps freedom meant acknowledging what had happened, then understanding it didn't have to determine my life. For all that assassins had pursued me through my dreams, I was still alive.

I could still look into the future and find it unwritten, just as I stared over the cliffs that afternoon, watching the sky meet the waves. What must the Caribs have thought, as they prepared to jump from the same spot? Perhaps that the remainder of their existence would not be momentary, but an infinite thing measured in half-seconds and heart-beats stretching before them further than they could count.

So they leaped. In tears and silence, pride and fear. Fathers, sisters, howling babies. Each of them glimpsing again the verdure of the forest, the outline of a lover's face at night, the thrumming of rain on rooftops and how, just before dawn, in the moment between the end of night and the new day, the island and its creatures would seem to catch their breath collectively, in silence, even the wind drawing still.

So they leaped. The span of their lives running before them in unbound specificity. And it appeared to the Caribs that they might remain poised above the waves for ever. Falling without landing they turned through the sky. Turned through the sky like black gold of the sun.